Gordon

SHAKESPEARIAN COMEDY

SHAKESPEARIAN COMEDY

AND OTHER STUDIES

BY

GEORGE GORDON

OXFORD UNIVERSITY PRESS

Oxford University Press, Amen House, London E.C.4
GLASGOW NEW YORK TORONTO MELBOURNE WELLINGTON
BOMBAY CALCUTTA MADRAS KARACHI LAHORE DACCA
CAPE TOWN SALISBURY NAIROBI IBADAN ACCRA
KUALA LUMPUR HONG KONG

FIRST PUBLISHED 1944; REPRINTED 1945
REPRINTED LITHOGRAPHICALLY IN GREAT BRITAIN
AT THE UNIVERSITY PRESS, OXFORD
FROM SHEETS OF THE SECOND IMPRESSION
1947, 1953, 1961, 1965

PREFACE

GEORGE GORDON'S work on Shakespeare began soon after he became a Fellow of Magdalen in 1907, with an edition of selected plays for school use, and the poet was thereafter the frequent subject of his discourse, as Professor of English Literature at Leeds (1913–22) and Merton Professor of English at Oxford (1922–8), in lectures given during a visit to Norway and Sweden (1924) and at the Royal Institution (1925–6), as Clark Lecturer at Trinity College, Cambridge (1934), and finally as Professor of Poetry at Oxford (1935–8).

Himself a humorist, he was perhaps happiest in dealing with the Comedies. His treatment of these was constantly revised, and brought ultimately to a high state of lucidity and finish. The present selection is intended to give him at his ripest. The lectures on 'What is Comedy?' and 'Shakespeare's Answer' represent a careful rewriting for Oxford on topics already handled at Cambridge. From the Clark lectures themselves are taken the passages on 'The Dislike of Comedy', 'Shakespeare the Englishman', 'Shakespeare's Periods', 'The World of the Comedies', 'Shakespeare's Women', and 'Shakespeare's Clowns'. The lecture on *King Lear* was given at Oxford in 1937. On the *Othello* and on the revision of his early introduction to *The Tempest*, Gordon was working, almost up to the time of his death on 12 March 1942. The essay on 'Shakespeare's English', based on a lecture at the Royal Institution, was originally published (1928) by the Society for Pure English. This, too, was a subject constantly in Gordon's mind from an early date. He was still making collections on it in 1938.

I am responsible for the arrangement and editing of the

studies, as they now appear. Before the material came into my hands, much valuable work had already been done on it by Drs. R. W. Chapman and C. T. Onions and Mr. R. H. New, in elucidation of Gordon's difficult and often revised script.

1 July 1943 E. K. CHAMBERS

CONTENTS

I

WHAT IS COMEDY?

COMEDY has not been well treated by the philosophers. She started as a Cinderella of the Muses, and something of a Cinderella she has remained. All the weight of the philosophical criticism of the forms of drama has been directed on Tragedy, and the exhausted analyst, from Aristotle onwards, has generally been content to deal with Comedy in a postscript, or by that unsatisfactory method known as the method of reference. Make the necessary alterations, we are told, and almost everything that has been said of Tragedy may be applied to Comedy. But what *are* the necessary alterations? *Mutatis mutandis* is an important expression, and an ablative absolute will always be respectable; but we remain, on those terms, where we were. Even the best of our essayists, our freest minds, tend to succumb, in this matter, like the philosophers. 'I have confined my observations', says Charles Lamb, at the conclusion of a famous paper, 'to the tragic parts of Shakespeare. It would be no very difficult task'—they all say that—'to extend the enquiry to his comedies; and to shew why Falstaff, Shallow, Sir Hugh Evans, and the rest, are equally incompatible with stage representation.'

Some attempts have indeed been made, in the last half-century or so, to supply this persistent omission, and, at the moment, Comedy—its nature, its habits, and function—is engaging the attention of a number of our younger critics. They have turned to it, naturally enough, after the immense addition of our fathers and grandfathers to the study of Tragedy, and especially Shakespearian Tragedy. Criticism to-day is in considerable and not unhealthy reaction from that school of which Mr. Bradley's *Shakespearean Tragedy* is the last and most impressive monument. It looks round, also, for fresh work; and it is otherwise attracted rather to Comedy than to Tragedy by the circumstances of our time. Tragedy, both in the composition and the devoted study of it, demands some settled faith; and of that the stock at present is not plentiful.

I cannot find—and I have tried—that the new lights on Comedy, and on what we must *not*, apparently, call the Comic Spirit, yet help us much. I doubt, also, if I can add particularly to their fitful, petulant, and sometimes angry illuminations. They seem to be united in resentment at the idea that Laughter should be attached to Comedy, as in any sense its end and object—an attitude which would have surprised most of its European masters. But it cannot have escaped you how very serious some of our new schools of criticism are. They seem even to make an art and profession of that particular form of incongruity—itself an element of the comic—which consists in being studiously more solemn and more elaborate, the less the subject seems to invite such treatment. Let us respect all honest and independent inquiry, and let us agree that on serious subjects there are times when we cannot be *too* serious. But let us beware, also, let us quite particularly beware, of *les Tartuffes de la critique*.

Modern discussions of Comedy in this country still start—if only in scorn and repugnance—from the famous essays of Meredith and Bergson, of which the first, on *The Idea of Comedy*, is forty-seven years old, and the other, on *Laughter*, thirty-five. I propose in this lecture, with Shakespearian Comedy in my mind, to look again at those highly interesting but now ageing productions. Though abundantly criticized, they have not yet, so far as I am aware, been replaced or superseded by any critical analyses of equal power.

Meredith, being an Englishman, takes, as might have been expected, a less strict and contracted view of the subject of Comedy than Bergson, though his special taste in comic drama is much the same. He holds firmly that Comedy, High Comedy—and you will note the question-begging epithet—appeals to the intelligence pure and simple—or rather, pure and not simple—and aims not at our ribs or armpits but at our heads. This Comedy, therefore, is critical, and its main use is to teach the world what ails it. This it does by the exercise of an intelligence 'keen-edged', and 'by nature merciless'. Molière, for example, the supreme executant in this mode, 'strips folly to the skin', and upon vice wields a 'shrieking scourge'. Yet in all this there is no contempt or anger. 'Derisive laughter thwarts the comic idea.' The laughter of Comedy is 'impersonal, and of unrivalled politeness, nearer a smile'. The victim is flayed, that is to say—but without heat, quite impersonally—while over all the Comic Spirit, that 'sly and wise emanation' eyeing us from aloft, offers its 'slim feasting smile', and on the fit company of ladies and gentlemen, in their exquisite social equality, showers down those now notorious 'volleys of silvery laughter'.

In all this Meredith was well aware that he was describing an ideal of Comedy neither familiar to this island nor very congenial to it. What Bergson only just catches sight of at the end of *his* essay—I mean, the more generous and kindly possibilities of Laughter, of Laughter and Comedy—Meredith, as a fellow countryman of Shakespeare, must have been conscious of throughout. But he fails or refuses to take account of them in his definition, or to adjust the levels of his dissertation to their richer contours. He has very deliberately narrowed and specialized the idea of Comedy, firstly, because he honestly believed that the purest essence of Comedy could not be otherwise obtained, and secondly, because he seems to have been equally convinced that this essence of Comedy, as he found it in the classical theatre of France, was only uncongenial to the English stage, because we were not yet sufficiently civilized to stand it. This second, and social, motive of his essay is never forgotten by Meredith, and is the explanation, if not the excuse, of most of his critical confusions and extravagances. The year, remember, was 1877. In this essay Meredith is missionary as well as critic, and sometimes the missionary takes command. He is an ally of Matthew Arnold, still conducting, under the same banner of lucidity and reason and the classic doctrine of the pure intelligence, his long warfare against English Philistinism, against our island crudities. This quintessential Comedy, on the description of which Meredith lavished an almost vulgar brilliance, was regarded by its panegyrist even more as a social test and exercise than as an artistic ideal. By its capacity for this kind of Comedy—by its ability to endure, in mixed companies of men and women, 'the calm and curious eye' of what he calls the Comic Spirit, he was prepared to judge a civilization. And he thought it high time that his fellow Victorians should be told so.

Well—no doubt we need such shining onslaughts, and our way, when they come, is to praise them, to meet our punishment with applause. But why, amidst all this brilliant wrist-play, this pinking of our insular heartiness, why is our flushed and agile swordsman so uncomfortable? Why does he keep breaking off to look over his shoulder? Because, having emptied Comedy of so much that, in England at any rate, we think native to it—having slimmed it to French taste—he is haunted by the mighty forces he has expelled. Humour for one, and the hearty and generous laughter that accompanies it. For such laughter is, by definition, not thoughtful enough for the select enclosure of High Comedy. Let us emulate rather the 'mentally digestive laugh' of the 'polished Frenchman'. I should like to have heard Charles Lamb on this subject. He was roused once, on much smaller provocation, by a remark of his friend Manning.

What you assert concerning the actors of Paris, that they exceed our comedians, 'bad as ours are', is *impossible*. Their fine gentlemen, in what is called genteel comedy, may possibly be more brisk and *dégagé*—; but have any of them the power to move *laughter* in *excess*? or can a Frenchman *laugh*? Can they batter at your judicious ribs till they shake, nothing loth to be shaken? This is John Bull's contention, and it shall be mine. You are Frenchified.

Meredith had already abjured this rib-shaking just *because* it was John Bullish, but could not escape a recurrent uneasiness when he thought of it. He denies the English much, but he acknowledges, rather late—too late for the frame of his essay—that they are noble humorists; and (in a burst of concession) that the great humorists have an embrace of contrasts beyond the scope of *his* comic poet; that the stroke of the great humorist is world-wide, with lights of Tragedy in his laughter; that the larger natures are even *distinguished* by the great breadth of their power of laughter. These concessions reach their climax when, in apparent defiance of his whole argument, he crowns, as the unapproachable monarchs of the world of Comedy, two men, Shakespeare and Cervantes. There they stand, as he places them, between Aristophanes and Molière, and are credited with a richer laugh than either, because it is 'the laughter of heart and mind in one'.

The urban negations, the genteel and intellectual avoidances, that went to the making of Meredith's specific Idea of Comedy, could not be more strikingly confessed. From that dramatic and social abstraction Shakespeare and Shakespearian Comedy are excluded by definition. It is *not* because they are devoid of thoughtful laughter, that laughter of the mind which true Comedy should arouse. They are acknowledged to have that. The trouble is that they have so much more; that they have something else as well which seems particularly inconvenient—the laughter of the heart—and, more baffling still, that these two, the laughter of heart and mind, are so often, in Shakespearian Comedy, inextricably interfused.

It is perhaps idle to ask why Meredith did not frame a definition of Comedy ample enough to embrace its most superb examples, and, by differentiation, develop and expound to his heart's content that particular species or specialization of it, which he thought most suitable to a refined society, and most likely to civilize the English comic stage. As it is, he is in a critical disorder throughout, and when he has gone half-way becomes conscious of it. My explanation, as I have said, is that he thought of his discourse chiefly as a social tract, a message to the times, and that he sharpened the point of his not unsalutary deliverance at the expense of his subject. His chief embarrassment is Shakespeare, who is an embarrassment, indeed, to all theorists. Where to put him, if the Comic Spirit was to remain at all tidy, keep her town clothes intact, and retain her heartless well-groomed smile and that detestable silvery laugh? What to do with a man who *will* paint humanity rather than manners; whose types break contract by immediately coming alive and taking their freedom—their whimsical freedom—as men and women? Meredith breaks off at one point—deserts his special theme—in order to praise Shakespeare, and with a novelist's admiration of his power of life-giving.

Shakespeare is a well-spring of characters which are saturated with the comic spirit; with more of what we will call blood-life than is to be found anywhere out of Shakespeare; and they are of this world, but they are of this world enlarged to our embrace by imagination, and by great poetic imagination. They are, as it were, creatures of the woods and wilds, not in walled towns, not grouped and toned to pursue a comic exhibition of the narrower world of society. Jacques, Falstaff and his regiment, the varied troop of Clowns, Malvolio, Sir Hugh Evans and Fluellen—marvellous Welshmen!—Benedick and Beatrice, Dogberry, and the rest, are subjects of a special study in the *poetically comic*.

It is a handsome evasion—and all the apology Meredith could offer for having refused the utmost embraces of his theme. This special study still remains to be written.

Meredith, in the passage I have quoted, heightens, for

obvious reasons, the pre-urban quality of Shakespeare's characters: 'as it were, creatures of the woods and wilds, not in walled towns'. He must excuse himself for having excluded such superb creatures from his chosen kingdom of Comedy. Yet there is much truth in his exaggeration. It extracts a quality which he had earlier noted as probably English. 'It has been suggested', he says, as an explanation of the reluctant appetite of his countrymen for High Comedy, 'that they have not yet spiritually comprehended the significance of living in society; for who are cheerfuller, brisker of wit, in the fields—and as explorers, colonizers, backwoodsmen? They are happy in rough exercise, and also in complete repose.' Walter Raleigh, in a well-known lecture on *Shakespeare and England*, has made admirable play with this idea.

New institutions, he says, do not flourish in England. The town is a comparatively modern innovation; it has never, so to say, caught on. Most of our schemes of town planning are schemes for pretending that you live in the country. This is one of the most persistent of our many hypocrisies. Wherever working people inhabit a street of continuous red-brick cottages, the names that they give to their homes are one long catalogue of romantic lies. The houses have no gardens, and the only prospect that they command is the view of over the way. But read their names—The Dingle, The Elms, Pine Grove, Windermere, The Nook, The Nest. All this is reflected in Shakespeare. He knew the country, and he knew the town; and he has not left it in doubt which was the cherished home of his imagination. He preferred the fields to the streets; but the Arcadia of his choice is not agricultural or even pastoral; it is rather a desert island, or the uninhabited stretches of wild and woodland country . . . When he indulges himself, as he did in his latest plays, you must look for him in the wilds; whether in the road near the shepherd's cottage, or in the cave among the mountains of Wales, or on the seashore in the Bermudas.

Perhaps Meredith, in excluding those romantic forces, those hobnails and tanned faces, from his chosen salon of dramatic art, showed prudence. He at least lets them camp in the courtyard.

From Meredith to Bergson is an easy transition, a movement within the same field. Bergson asks the prior question: what in fact the Comic is, of which Comedy is the finished dramatic form. If it be also asked how much his answer helps us as students of Shakespeare, I must answer, 'Directly very little, but indirectly a good deal'. For first he lays down like Meredith that Laughter as such appeals only to the intelligence —'to the intelligence pure and simple'—and points for confirmation to that absence of feeling which, he asserts—to me strangely—is the usual accompaniment of Laughter. And we laugh at what? As a rule at some person or incident out of keeping, in certain classifiable ways, with our social mode and habit. Some element of rigidity, inelasticity, or automatism in a character; some suggestion of the mechanical incrusted (as he puts it) on the living, seen, for example, in all the shades of absentmindedness (that stock affair of Comedy), and reaching, in the richer comic types, to a kind of daylight somnambulism pursued on occasion with the logic of a dream—this, it appears, is the common groundwork of the socially laughable, and can be illustrated through the whole gamut of the comic, from a man chasing his hat to Don Quixote. Bergson does, very ingeniously, so illustrate it. And the purpose of the laughter? The purpose of the laughter is *corrective*: it asserts instructively, and without benevolence—for such laughter cannot be kind, no laughter can—the surprise of society that anyone should so isolate himself, and with such unconsciousness of his oddity, from the ordinary responses, the customary give and take, of the community in which he lives.

Such, in closest summary, is Bergson's analysis, and, if fairly applied, it *does* give some results. The great tribe of the Dogberries and Verges are accounted for: complete automatism, according to Bergson, 'is only recorded in Mr.

Official'. Vanity, Self-love, all the Pedantries (with their unnumbered flock of comic impersonations) submit to this anatomy, and Don Quixote is deftly classified as the greatest of all the somnambulists—with Malvolio, may I suggest, as a minor and parochial brother of his house. Yet how much in our English Comedy is recalcitrant to Bergson's treatment! That analysis of the Comic can scarcely be applauded which leaves Falstaff outside, or accounts for nothing but his paunch.

I am afraid that M. Bergson has most of the defects as well as the signal merits of the Parisian mind. Whatever his sense of humour, he has none of simple fun, and is bounded in his view of Comedy by the classical stage of France—by that comedy of types of which Molière is the acknowledged master, and to which Shakespearian Comedy offers the boldest antithesis. How otherwise can he define Laughter as by its nature devoid of feeling, or if tinged at all with feeling, then unbenevolent? There is friendly as well as unfriendly laughter, as we rude island readers of Shakespeare know; nor can anything exceed in that way the kindness, the rejoicing and protective kindness, which we feel for the humorists and grotesques of the Shakespearian stage. So little is our laughter on those occasions a social gesture, a social corrective, a flick of the whip to bring anomalies into the social fold—so little do we feel this that, on the contrary, we would not have them altered by a hair, and desire nothing so much as that they should go on *ad infinitum* being precisely the absurd anomalies they are. The reason for this, though it escaped M. Bergson, is that Shakespeare habitually creates not types, but men and women—that they are as real to us to-day as when Shakespeare made them—and have acquired in our companionable affections a historic as well as a dramatic being. There is a passage in Hegel's *Aesthetik* which is of interest here. Hegel especially selects, as examples of Shakespeare's power, Falstaff, and—what seems an odd choice for a philosopher—Stephano, Trinculo, and Pistol. Why? Because what he admired most in Shakespeare was what he admired in Dante and in Don Quixote: the strength of the individual character, what G. M. Hopkins calls *inscape*, the resistance of the character to all outward pressure of conformity. Like the people in Dante, like Don Quixote, they are each an intelligence. Hegel has put his finger on a truth. The very essence of these characters is their successful and approved resistance to that outward pressure of social adaptation which, according to Bergson's theory, and to Meredith's also, it is the business of Comedy to exert.

Towards the end of his essay, two or three pages from the end, M. Bergson had for a moment a misgiving. Up to that point he had consistently regarded Laughter as 'first and foremost a means of correction'. But how, in that case—he at last admits the question—how is it that our *first* impression of the laughable does not, in fact, agree with this?

> The comic character, he confesses, is often one with whom, to begin with, our mind, or rather our body, sympathises. By this is meant that we put ourselves for a very short time in his place, adopt his gestures, words, and actions, and if amused by anything laughable in him, invite him, in imagination, to share his amusement with us; in fact, we treat him as a playfellow.

How admirable of M. Bergson to have seen this at last! He has covered in this sentence more than half the distance from Harpagon to Falstaff. He now notes, growing wiser and wiser, that there is in laughter 'a movement of relaxation': and what is the reason for that? It is to be found, perhaps, he supposes, in the comic character himself, who, bored with the business of adapting and re-adapting himself to the society of which he is a member, 'slackens in the attention that is due to life'.

> In some way or another he is *absent*, away from his work, taking it easy. He abandons social convention . . . Our first impulse is to

accept the invitation to take it easy. For a short time, at all events, we join in the game. And that relieves us from the strain of living.

Surely this is excellent! M. Bergson, no longer merely critical and prim, but with at last some of the strong air of Eastcheap in his lungs, M. Bergson is now *bowling* along, and his theory of Comedy, at this generous rate, will presently be ample enough to embrace the comic world, to enclose in its orbit our Shakespeare as well as Molière. So it might, if he had only gone on, but at this point, growing frightened, he stops dead. He was alarmed, we may suppose, at the wide prospect opened up, just as his essay was concluding, of quite another kind of laughter and quite another kind of comedy—of a mood so merely joyous and so wholly relieved of all social responsibility—so Shakespearian, in fact—as to bring in question the ultimate validity of his whole critical construction—as an account, at any rate, of Comedy in general. Could it be that he had generalized on insufficient evidence, from one type of Comedy to all?

Thus faced with the possibility of having to rewrite his book, he acts with decision and dispatch. That state of joyous and irresponsible release which some comic characters induce in us, though it cannot unfortunately be denied, is yet of short duration. The sympathy one feels for them is 'a very fleeting one'. We have been caught unawares, through some lapse in attention. 'Thus, a stern father may at times forget himself and join in some prank his child is playing, only to check himself at once in order to correct it.' Was there ever a more determined travesty? That lapse in attention, that catching unawares, that mood of delighted and irresponsible surrender to the motley, all of which are regarded by Bergson as momentary weaknesses in our critical rôle of spectator, are surely, in fact, in the Shakespearian order of things, of the very essence of the comic idea! But Bergson is now adamant, and draws in his skirts, as if shocked by these glimpses of the vulgar roominess of a comic world which is not his own. He raps out once more, as if for personal reassurance, the neat formulae with which he began: that 'laughter is, above all, a corrective', that 'being intended to humiliate, it must make a painful impression on the person against whom it is directed', that 'by laughter Society avenges itself for the liberties taken with it; and that it would fail in its object, if it bore the stamp of sympathy or kindness'. Is it not disappointing, I ask, to see a philosopher so flatly refuse his chance of universality?

The difficulty is real, of course, and it is here, if anywhere, that modern criticism may expect to improve on earlier analyses. So long and so firmly has the corrective or satiric type of Comedy been established as the type *par excellence*, that even Hazlitt, you may remember, had misgivings. 'It is perhaps the fault', he says, 'of Shakespeare's comic muse that it is too goodnatured and magnanimous. We sympathize with his characters more often than we laugh at them. His ridicule wants the sting of ill-nature. Falstaff himself is so great a joke rather for his being so huge a mass of enjoyment than of absurdity.'

I suspect that the difficulty is largely one of terminology. The subject has not yet been submitted to a comprehensive enough analysis. How can we define, for example, with any competence, the nature and species of Comedy, when the ultimate test of its nature—its relations with Tragedy—is still so uncertain in the writings of all the critics? The close kinship of Shakespearian Comedy with Tragedy is apparent to every reader, and indeed the traditional terminology breaks down so badly that Mr. Shaw can speak, I think without flippancy, of *Coriolanus* as Shakespeare's best comedy, and others of *The Tempest* as, of course, essentially a tragedy. The difficulty is apparent in M. Bergson's essay. It is a just and serious criticism of that work that it contains hardly any definition of Comedy which could not, with the slightest shifting of emphasis, be made to serve as a definition of Tragedy.

There is a further and temporal difficulty. We do not now laugh just where our forefathers laughed, or we laugh where they were grave. Henry Irving used to play Richard III as a sort of Polichinello, with the richest vein of humour. A serious and even tragic dignity has been read for a century into the character of Shylock—and even into that of Sir Peter Teazle—into those of Tartuffe and George Dandin. On the other hand, in these last fifty years, we have not always endured Tragedy so well as our grandfathers, and like the sting taken out. Forbes Robertson's was the most acceptable Hamlet of his time because he insisted on the sunny side of the man, and generally, as Walkley said, 'gave Elsinore a thorough airing'. Clearly all the categories of our dramatic classifications are shifting. In time, if Anatole France is right, they may disappear altogether. In *Sur la Pierre Blanche* he pictures the world in the year A.D. 2070, when Europe will have converted itself into one vast Socialist Federation, and conjectures that the Theatre will by then have become almost exclusively musical. An exact knowledge of reality and a life without violence will have made the human race almost indifferent to Tragedy, while the unification of classes and total sex-equality will have deprived Comedy of nearly all its subject-matter.

Well, that is some way off, and I am glad to think concerns none of us now.

II

SHAKESPEARE'S ANSWER

In an earlier and somewhat arid discourse I was concerned with the discordance between the orthodox satiric or corrective theory of Comedy and the practice of Shakespeare. An examination of the two most famous expositions of that theory, one English and one French, disclosed its delusive neatness as an account of Comedy in general, and revealed also the discomfort of its eminent expositors when they allowed themselves to reflect on the extravagant cost of their critical tidiness, on the richness and wholesomeness of the comic forces which they were excluding. A theory of Comedy, or of Comedy *par excellence*, which relegates, and is bound to relegate, most of Shakespeare's comic world to an appendix, stands, clearly, on too narrow a basis, at any rate for English use.

One suggestion was that Shakespeare is too poetic for Comedy proper. Comedy deals with familiar surroundings and with society as it exists; but Shakespeare the romantic habitually does neither. There is, of course, much truth in this. Recall that romantic world in which Shakespeare is happiest—the world of his comedies and young people—that incomparable rainbow mixture of Old England and Utopia—and you will observe that most of these plays begin with some artificial seclusion or segregation from the world. The curtain goes up; and at once, or in a scene or two, the door is shut on ordinary life. Except in *The Comedy of Errors* and *The Merchant of Venice*, where the play opens on a public mart, hardly anybody goes to business in these Shakespearian latitudes, or seems to be obliged to get up at any particular time—though, on the whole, except for the drinkers, all

Shakespeare's people like the morning. The scene being staged for Love, it is essential that its young people should be idle, should have time on their hands. No enemy of Love like work! Everyone of importance lives on his or her estate; or in Arcadia—where there are no clocks, and everybody helps everybody else. It is a world of delicious make-believe: of Academes, Illyrias, and Forests of Arden—of seaside Bohemias or desert islands. Even when the scene is most real—when the postal address is known—it is still romantic and Utopian: for what, as we know, is Verona, what is Padua, but 'somewhere in Italy'? And Italy, to the Shakespearian young, was the Worldly Paradise, where a Lucentio might hopefully look for 'love in idleness'.

The first, or almost the first, of these deliberate segregations is in the comedy of *Love's Labour's Lost*. The Prince and his two male friends forswear women and the facts of life, and retire to the seclusion of their own thoughts: to a kind of anti-feminist retreat, furnished with every bachelor convenience. Even if, as is alleged, this fiction is topical, and was intended to make fun of a preciosity of the time, it attracted Shakespeare as a pleasant vanity—one of the aristocratic sports of the Renaissance. It answers, evidently, to an ancient instinct. Long before the private Academes of Italy there were the monastic Academes of the religious, whose sign was the Cross; and the mixed monasteries of the worldly, in that mythical Garden of the Middle Ages whose sign was a flower—the Garden of the Rose. Perhaps the best model of all these aristocratic pleasure parties—these Colleges of *Thelēma*—of 'As You Like It'—is the Florentine Garden of Boccaccio, with its company of ladies and gentlemen telling their witty and courtly stories while the plague of life rumbled grimly outside. Shakespeare accepts the game with all its affectations, because they are *poetical* affectations; but of course he is not deceived. Even if the poetry comes first with him, he never forgets the work of Comedy. For what are they all, these charming lay societies, but attempts to reach Utopia on the cheap? I say, on the cheap, because what these attractive worldlings will not face, as Shakespeare well knew, is the *price* of Utopia. That price is constant, and is nothing less than a change of mind and heart. Shakespeare accepts these affectations—and when he has extracted the last ounce of poetry from them—but not till then—up goes his hand, crash goes the merry bomb of Comedy, and they are exploded in thin air. All he asks is a gentleman's park or a forest somewhere—and for three acts his young people walking about in it. If Life, which they believe they have eluded—if Life the traitor, with all its duties and responsibilities, is not already busy among them—Shakespeare will see to it that he finds a way in. Sooner or later, to these Young Utopians on the cheap, Shakespearian Comedy presents the bill. We have our own failures. We still form Reading Parties which are no more successful than that other Reading Party in *Love's Labour's Lost*, and often enough for the same reason. Every College in this University[1] was originally such an attempt; and the result is now known. Sooner or later, as in the comedies of Shakespeare and the *Arcadia* of Sidney, the God of Marriage erects his straggling monuments; and we tumble from the clouds, with all the Rosalinds and Orlandos and other Young Utopians, into a world of taxes, and villas, and perambulators. To every Academe its North Oxford.

I know nothing more artistically interesting or more truly Elizabethan than to see Shakespeare at work on this fiction of segregation—on this deliciousness of Nowhere; to see him set it up in the pride of fancy, and undermine it with the pride of life. For in Shakespeare—however fantastic and Utopian the fiction may be—Life always comes in and claims its due. Partly, as I said, this is good Elizabethan, for there never was a more Utopian or a more practical age. It is their peculiar mixture, their elixir: and perhaps it is the secret of

[1] Oxford.

every great age. Partly it is the healthy conscience of Shakespeare, of a man who all his life, headache or no headache, had to work for his living—and to maintain, among all his dreams and fancies, a steady balance with reality. Shakespeare was never permitted, like so many of our later poets, to practise the art of segregation in his own life, and—like Coleridge, Wordsworth, and Shelley (to name no others)—be a gifted pensioner on society. If it is true, as I think it is, that of all that group of a century ago the most Shakespearian figure is Charles Lamb, then I ask you to go further with me and to agree that not the least of the reasons for this resemblance is that Lamb daily, and at the same hours, went about his business, and worked for his living. Whoever, still keeping his dreams, stoops to the necessities of life, and shoulders his burden, has very singular rewards.

Shakespeare, then, poetic as he is, does not neglect the work of Comedy. But it is said that he is too good-natured, too kind for Comedy. Comedy has a mission, and in the interests of society must have the courage to be cruel, to use the lash. In the art of cruelty, and in whipcracking generally, it must be admitted that Shakespeare is defective. Not that he is without satire: he makes fun, of course, like all comedians, of the follies of his time: *Love's Labour's Lost*, it begins to be known and has always been suspected, is as topical as Gilbert's *Patience*. But hardly even of that rather exceptional play can it be said that satire, in the end, is its principal motive. Poetry and cheerfulness are always breaking in. One is conscious, from time to time, in many of the masterpieces of social Comedy, of the author as *censor morum*, as the representative of sane society, of *les honnêtes hommes*, flicking his whip, pinking his man. But we have, I make bold to say, no such feeling in reading Shakespeare: if his characters are corrected, the correction seems not to come from some external power: they seem to do it for one another. If exposures are made, it is still a family affair. Shakespeare's comedies, regarded purely as Comedy, present us with a holy war, conducted without malice or bloodshed on Egotism, Sentimentalism, Pedantry, and Self-importance: on precisely those weaknesses and follies, in short, which, without being criminal, make bad citizens and bad neighbours—tiresome husbands and tiresome wives—which make men and women unsociable, and unfit for the friendly purposes of life. They say to Life, these people, like peevish children, that they 'won't play', and are laughed by Shakespearian Comedy into the game.

Let me take a slender but typical example from the class of Egotistic Lovers. It cannot have escaped you how very egotistic and unsocial lovers can be. They have a roughish time of it in Shakespeare's comedies, but all, let me remind you, within the family. We are privileged, in *Much Ado*, to see the first dawning of Claudio's passion for Hero; and *whom* should he confide in but Benedick his friend? It was a rash step. For it is a law of Shakespearian Comedy—part of its family code—that every excess of egotism or sentiment shall be treated as an illness; and first aid, not always of the gentlest, shall be instantly applied.

Claudio. Benedick, didst thou note the daughter of Signior Leonato?
Bene. I noted her not; but I looked on her.
Claudio. Is she not—a—modest young lady?
Bene. [*looking more closely at him*]. Do you question me, as an honest man should do, for my simple true judgement; or would you have me speak after my custom, as being a professed tyrant to their sex?
Claudio. No; I pray thee; speak in sober judgement.
Bene. Why, i' faith, methinks she's too low for a high praise, too brown for a fair praise, and too little for a great praise; only this commendation I can afford her, that were she other than she is, she were unhandsome, and being no other but as she is—I do not like her.
Claudio. Thou thinkest I am in sport. I pray thee tell me truly how thou likest her.

Bene. Would you buy her, that you inquire after her?
Claudio. Can the world buy such a jewel?
Bene. [*in the same tone*]. Yea, and a case to put it into.

A little unkind, perhaps, but how *good* for Claudio! And the game is not one-sided. It is tit for tat. Claudio will have his chance at Benedick, when *he* goes the same reluctant way: and so, in Shakespeare's manner, every excess acts physician to every other. It is first aid all round.

There are also—if I may take another example of this family treatment—there are also the *Verbalists*, the *Fine and Clever Talkers*, whose brains have gone to their heads. Shakespeare in private life, was, on unimpeachable evidence, a great talker himself, and there can have been nothing about this interesting weakness that he did not know. But Life, as he knew still better—as all women have always known—is not run by clever talk—is, on the contrary, often impeded by it. In the comedies of Shakespeare nearly all the principal offenders in this way are *men*: it was a weakness of the age; and it is noticeable that their punishment and their cure are generally placed by Shakespeare in the hands of women. I need recall only Biron in *Love's Labour's Lost* and Jaques in *As You Like It*.

Shakespeare's women, of course, can play this verbal game themselves, and do, in fact, as we know, play it admirably; but only, as a rule, sufficiently to protect themselves and keep the ball rolling: it is generally to be suspected that their hearts are not wholly in it. If they are interested in a man, it is very often not so much what he *says* that interests them, as what he does *not* say, and might perhaps have said. All Shakespeare's gentlewomen have a gift of silence; and, unprovoked, are naturally of few words.

Shallow. Here comes fair Mistress Anne. Would I were young for your sake, Mistress Anne.
Anne. The dinner is on the table.

There is a striking passage in *Cymbeline*, where Imogen is forced by the importunity of Cloten to state her full mind about his proposals. She does so, and then—even to Cloten—apologizes for it, feeling it to be out of character:

> I am much sorry, sir,
> You put me to forget a lady's manners,
> By being so verbal.

It is, as you know, a jest of all time that *women* are the talkative sex; and all the jest books of Shakespeare's day were full of it. It shows the admirable perception of Shakespeare that he was not deceived. Whatever washerwomen may do, Shakespeare's *grandes dames*, his Elizabethan great ladies, unless provocation drives them, speak quietly and to the point.

Shakespeare's comedies, I need hardly say, are very far from being of equal merit. He wrote most of them in the first ten years of his working life, and when he began, the great age of Elizabethan literature was just preparing to flower. Of the miracle of those ten years in our dramatic literature alone, of that leap from crudity to artistic excellence, and to an excellence by no means naive, but often technically most elaborate, no historian of our literature has ever found or ever will find a satisfactory explanation. This sudden enlightenment and efflorescence is best studied in Shakespeare, and only familiarity could restrain a deserved and perpetual astonishment that *The Comedy of Errors*, let us say, should be separated by not more than three or four years from *The Merchant of Venice* and *Romeo and Juliet*, and by not more than eight or nine from the mellow maturity of *As You Like It* and *Twelfth Night*.

Our first interest in these early comedies is chiefly, then, that they are Shakespeare's, and that he wrote so very much better comedies later on. It is a privilege to see genius growing up—to catch it, as it were, between man and boy—or, as Beatrice would say, with three hairs on its chin. But there is a further and more technical interest in these early plays. Shakespeare, above almost every other comic dramatist of his rank, used the theatrical stock-in-trade of his time, and in his earlier plays—since the rest of the cupboard is barer—the anatomy of these conventions is more easily seen. Take, for example, *The Two Gentlemen of Verona.* All the stage-tricks of the comic and romantic drama of western Europe, some of them hoary with antiquity, are to be found there: the window and balcony, the inevitable serenade, the rope-ladder, the convenient Friar, outlaws and a forest. Julia, the first of a long line of Shakespearian heroines in hose and doublet, timidly starts a practice which is followed with more confidence by Viola, Rosalind, and Imogen, and in *The Merchant of Venice* not by one woman, but by all—a raid on the masculine wardrobe. Here also is to be met the first of those inimitable servingmen, half-valets, half-clowns, without whom no Shakespearian comedy is to be complete. Launce has many collaterals in the works of Shakespeare, each richer and more mouldy than the last: and when I say mouldy, I use it in an honourable sense, as of a cheese.

None of the stock characters and devices are peculiar to Shakespeare, or his own invention. He uses the old business over and over again, never tiring of it, apparently, nor his audience either; and we think of it as Shakespearian because he did it so much better than anyone else, and with an art so constantly improving not only upon his contemporaries but upon himself. In the end it is steeped in poetry, and in *The Tempest* passes away in a pageant not of this world.

This conservatism of Shakespeare, this contentment with the convention, goes deeper still, and affects the very postulates of his plays. Every play that ever was written begins with a request. It asks us to admit something. Suppose, says the dramatist, these people to have come together, and to be in these positions, let me show you what happens. Accept this hypothesis, and everything follows. Refuse it, and the play cannot go on. I am describing the first rule of the game. Shakespeare, in his comedies, usually asks a good deal of us—puts a strain on our credulity. And this is one of his disabilities, according to the critics, for the social and corrective mission of *la haute comédie*, or, as they call it, Comedy Proper.

Take an unvarnished example. If you have read *The Comedy of Errors*, you are aware of the monstrous improbability on which that play is founded. The pair of twins so exactly alike that even their mother cannot tell them apart—so much we are prepared to accept: it is well known that this may happen: and any dramatist or story-teller is entitled to get all the fun he can out of their mistaken identities. But Shakespeare is not content with this.

> That very hour, and in the self-same inn,
> A meaner woman was delivered
> Of such a burden, male twins, both alike.

The father of the first pair, somewhat struck by the circumstance—he calls it 'strange', being a rich man—buys the second pair from their parents, who were very poor, and brings them up to be attendants on his sons. What more is wanted? They take ship to go home; along comes the obedient storm of the romancer; the ship founders; the family is dispersed; rich twin sticks to poor twin, each in his pair—the dramatist waves his hand—twenty years have passed; and the play, ladies and gentlemen, he announces, is about to begin. The question is, shall we, revolted by these demands on our credulity, refuse the invitation, decline to walk up?

On this I would remark that, though Shakespeare never again asks quite so much of us, he continues to ask a good deal; and that a refusal on this ground alone to have any dealings with one of his comedies must logically be extended to others. Even in so mature and so masterly a play as

Twelfth Night we are presented, in the hypothesis, with a young lady—the central figure of the play—who puns with sailors on an unknown coast, having just been rescued from the water, and, as she supposed, seen her brother drowned before her eyes. Yet she puns. Nor is this all. With her clothes still dripping from her immersion she hastens to inquire who rules in these parts, and on being told, and hearing that the prince is a bachelor remarks, in effect, that this will do. She decides there and then to supplant the lady whom he courts.

Now, it is no doubt true that any ordinary woman in Viola's position—far from inventing, at such a moment, so ambitious a scheme of life—would have hastened to disclose herself to the nearest consul, and resume her journey. Because presumably she was *going* somewhere; and we know that she was penniless. On this way of thinking, the whole incident becomes monstrous and improbable. Viola is either inhuman or unreal. It is, however, the hypothesis of *Twelfth Night* that Viola does none of the things which an ordinary young woman would have done in her position, but forms instead, and instantly, the bold design which the play unravels. We *can*, of course, refuse this; but do we? It is asking a good deal more of us than most modern dramatists do; but something must be allowed to Romance. All fiction rests upon belief. Romance lives by it. Belief is its whole capital; and what does it matter if now and then the account is a little overdrawn? That bank, even to-day, can stand it. The dramatist like Shakespeare who goes beyond life to please us is entitled to a larger share of our credulity. It is our one way of paying him; and there is no price which, I believe, we pay so easily, or with half so good a will.

Of all our successful modern dramatists Barrie is likest to Shakespeare in this matter of hypothesis—the demands, I mean, which he makes on our preliminary good will. A play like *Dear Brutus* is very Shakespearian in this respect: in its smiling assumption that the audience will have faith. Not always easy for the modern playgoer—less easy, I imagine, than for the simpler-minded audiences of three hundred years ago. Yet—I must tell you a story. Two young naval officers, such nice fellows—so clearly the backbone of the country—once followed me out, at the end of a performance. 'A bit over my head, what?' said one, and the other, 'I liked the whistling'. It is probable that some such remarks may sometimes have been made as the crowd flocked out of the Globe Theatre after a first night of one of Shakespeare's comedies. 'The Masque was not ill done', or 'I liked the fencing'. There will always, of course, be readers, and even playgoers, who rebel, and query items in the dramatic bill of illusion. Lewis Carroll has left on record, in a letter to Ellen Terry, his inability to accept the hypotheses of *Much Ado*.

Now I'm going to put before you a 'Hero-ic' puzzle of mine, but please remember I do not ask for your solution of it, as you will persist in believing, if I ask your help in a Shakespearian difficulty, that I am only jesting! My difficulty is this: Why in the world did not Hero (or at any rate Beatrice on her behalf) prove an 'alibi' in answer to the charge? It seems certain that she did *not* sleep in her room that night; for how could Margaret venture to open the window and talk from it, with her mistress asleep in the room? It would be sure to wake her. Besides, Borachio says, after promising that Margaret shall speak with him out of Hero's chamber window, 'I will so fashion the matter that Hero shall be absent'. (How he could possibly manage any such thing is another difficulty, but I pass over that.) Well, then, granting that Hero has slept in some other room that night, why didn't she say so? When Claudio asked her: 'What man was he you talked with yesternight out at your window betwixt 12 and 1?' why didn't she reply, 'I talked with no man at that hour, my lord. Nor was I in my chamber yesternight, but in another, far from it, remote.' And this she could, of course, prove by the evidence of the housemaids, who must have known that she had occupied another room that night.

But even if Hero might be supposed to be so distracted as not to remember where she had slept the night before, or even whether she had slept anywhere, surely Beatrice had her wits about her; and when an arrangement was made, by which she was to lose, for one night, her twelve-months' bedfellow, is it conceivable that she didn't know *where* Hero passed the night? Why didn't she reply:

> But, good my lord, sweet Hero slept not there:
> She had another chamber for the nonce.
> 'Twas sure some counterfeit that did present
> Her person at the window, aped her voice,
> Her mien, her manners, and hath thus deceived
> My good Lord Pedro and his company?

With all these excellent materials for proving an 'alibi' it is incomprehensible that no one should think of it. If only there had been a barrister friend present to cross-examine Beatrice! 'Now, ma'am, attend to me, please, and speak up so that the jury can hear you. Where did you sleep last night? Where did Hero sleep? Will you swear that she slept in her own room? Will you swear that you do not know *where* she slept?' I feel inclined to quote old Mr. Weller and to say to Beatrice at the end of the play, 'Oh, Samivel, Samivel, vy vornt there a halibi'.

I am afraid there are few plays of Shakespeare which would survive this judge-and-jury method: few plays, indeed, of *any* dramatists of the older schools. Of course the answer is —as Lewis Carroll probably knew quite well—that such objections are vain cries from another world altogether, with which the world of the play has no treaty relations.

All lectures on Shakespeare's comedies tend to become lectures on Shakespeare's women, for in the comedies they have the front of the stage. Of most of Shakespeare's plays, as you are aware, no such feminine predominance can be asserted. It is absent from his English Histories, and from most of his Tragedies also. Whoever, when studying the Tragedies of Shakespeare, keeps his eyes sentimentally on the women—keeps thinking too much of Ophelia in *Hamlet* and of Cordelia in *King Lear*, of Lady Macbeth rather than of her husband, and of Desdemona rather than Othello—let us agree to thrust a slightly faded lily into that Shakespearian student's hand and push him gently out of doors.

In the world of the comedies, on the other hand, he may gratify his bent to the utmost. For it is true of most of Shakespeare's comedies, as it is of daily life, that where the woman is, there also, probably, is the root and heart of the matter. Shakespeare was a great student of women, and his portraits of women have never been surpassed: women of all ranks and ages—from the queen to the dairymaid—and from fifty to fifteen. The best of artists have their limits; but in this bright particular region Shakespeare would appear to have had none. From Cleopatra to Miranda—which I take to be very nearly the full span—he is equally at home, and has the whole range of femininity at his command.

I believe that the romance, the other-worldliness, the make-believe of the comedies, so favourable to his young heroines, may have been felt by Shakespeare as an escape from some of the other plays he was then writing—his plays from English history, plays of the medieval times, full of battle and murder and sudden death. You cannot read those history plays without noticing what a harsh and unfavourable soil they offer for the characteristic virtues and brighter graces of women. On that turbulent scene they have, indeed, as a rule, only one choice. They must either succumb to the violence of their men; or they must meet them quite primitively with what weapons they have by nature. The chief weapon of a woman, in violent times—perhaps at *all* times—is her tongue; and if that fails, it appears from these plays—such is the crudity of their civilization—that she can always scratch. Shakespeare's medieval women frequently mention their nails, their 'ten commandments', as they call them; but though they often *threaten* to scratch, as a rule it would seem to have been unnecessary. Their tongues are quite enough. The most hardened ruffians—all but Richard III—shrink from the precision of their insults as from the stings of adders. The head of the family of viragos is Queen Margaret ('Captain Margaret'), the wife of poor King Henry VI. When she appears, most of the men seem suddenly to remember that they had promised to be somewhere else. I will quote only one couplet of evidence:

> *Exeter.* Here comes the Queen . . . I'll steal away.
> *The King.* Exeter, so will I.

A formidable lady! He is her husband, mind you! The others mention their nails, and so does she, but when Queen Margaret means business, she uses the knife. It was a hard world for both women and children. Here and there, some woman finds it possible to remain womanly and survive; and it is for that reason that Queen Constance lives so graciously in our minds.

When we turn to the comedies of Shakespeare, we enter another world: a world of which the first quality is—what? With the English histories in my mind—as they were in Shakespeare's—I should say that its first quality is that it is a world made safe for women: a climate in which a girl can be happy and come to flower, in which the masculine element drops its voice. Certainly, whatever may have happened on the historical scene, here, in this land of Arcady, in this Utopia of Romance, Man, mere Man, lays down his arms. There is never any question who rules in these latitudes: it is Woman, Woman, all the time. I suppose no man ever grudged these glittering heroines, these Rosalinds, Violas, and Portias, their overpowering success. They so evidently deserve to win, and to put man in his place; for no more charming, witty, rebellious—and, I would remind you, level-headed—young women ever danced across a stage. Shakespeare's pen seems to move with a new grace and vivacity the moment one of them enters.

It is amusing to compare these young women of the

comedies with the young men who run after them; in other words, with their future husbands, for in Comedy, as you know, we all get our girls in the end. As the old play has it —'Jack hath Jill, And nought goes ill'. They are in love with each other, these young people—this couple and that couple; though the young women, as is only right and proper, are mostly rather slow to admit it. But mark, I would ask you, the difference in their behaviour! The young men are fine fellows, handsome, debonair, devoted; but it can hardly fail to have struck you how much better they are at talking than at doing anything! When any real business has to be done, when any difficult arrangement has to be made—who does it? Who makes it? Always the woman. The young men seem quite helpless, and while they are occupied in looking handsome and worthy of their parts, the women make the plans. Shakespeare is so consistent about this that I conceive he must have meant it. Turn to any comedy of Shakespeare's you like, from the first to the last: always it is the women who keep their heads, and see things through. I will take a prime example, out of many. I will take Portia, that well-known and very Shakespearian young lady, and those Venetian gentlemen who surround her in that play. What fumblers they all are compared to her! with just initiative enough to get into mischief, and not initiative enough to get out of it. She treats them all like rather likeable naughty children, which is very feminine of her, and what they deserve. They have their masculine pomposities, of course, and their fine public-meeting attitudes, and their great ideas.

Let me, at the risk of being elementary, recall the story. Young Bassanio, penniless, and in love with Portia, borrows the price of his trousseau from his friend Antonio, who in his turn, since times are hard, has borrowed it from Shylock the Jew, upon very strange terms. All goes well; Bassanio becomes the husband of Portia. Then news arrives that Antonio has been arrested and is in mortal trouble over that loan. Now, Bassanio is, as we say, a good fellow. He rushes back to Venice in the middle of his honeymoon, which alone was a considerable thing to do, and is present in court at the trial. He has, then, some useful suggestion to make, to save his friend, something practical to propose? On the contrary. Of anything practical he is as innocent as a child. He is only full of the very noblest impulses—for example, as follows:

> Antonio, I am married to a wife,
> Which is as dear to me as life itself;
> But life itself, my wife, and all the world,
> Are not with me esteem'd above thy life:
> I would lose all; ay, sacrifice them all,
> Here to this devil, to deliver you.

Now, that is a very fine sentiment, admirably expressed: and so helpful! To save his friend from the Jew—who (remember) has already refused all offers—he will consign himself and Portia to death: as if the Jew cared twopence what happened to *them*!

Hear now the answer of the Shakespearian woman, of the very lady, in fact, so generously sacrificed on the altar of friendship—sitting there, disguised in her lawyer's robes:

> Your wife would give you little thanks for that,
> If she were by, to hear you make the offer.

And yet, I dare say, she liked him all the better for it. So loyal a friend could hardly fail to make an excellent lover; and, firmly handled, might even ripen into a good husband. But it is Portia, not Bassanio, who sees the thing through, and saves Antonio. Compare Queen Elizabeth, in 1566, when angered by the persistence of the House of Commons in pressing marriage upon her. She flew out at her nobles, the Duke of Norfolk, the Earl of Pembroke, the Earl of Leicester. To Leicester she said that if all the world abandoned her, yet she had thought he would not have done so.

He swore that he would die at her feet. She retorted: 'Die at my feet! What has *that* to do with the matter?'

Considering what Shakespeare has done for them, I have always thought, and this is an old sermon of mine, that women have done singularly little for Shakespeare: I mean, in written interpretations of him and studies of his characters. On the stage, of course, they often interpret him admirably, and have done so any time these nearly 300 years; but off the stage, until almost the other day, hardly ever. We want both interpretations from them. I shall be reminded of Mrs. Jameson, Helena Faucit, and the rest, who *did* write on Shakespeare's women; and they were well enough in their way. But they are not nearly what I have in mind. His Comedies are a riot of feminine supremacy, a feminist revel. He has done women more honour than any other dramatist, except possibly Molière. And yet so few women have applied to his works those powers of analysis, peculiar to their sex, which they exercise daily in every drawing-room in Europe on the characters of their acquaintance. I can recall only one nineteenth-century Englishwoman who writes of Shakespeare's women as one woman in any drawing-room will talk of another—Mary Coleridge (a relative of the poet), who died in 1907; and she wrote nothing deliberate on Shakespeare, but only scraps, here and there, in diaries and letters, most femininely. She can tell me things that no man can tell me: about Isabella, for example, in *Measure for Measure*, and that desperate marriage of Mariana: 'The real Isabella could not have borne the thought of any woman being married to Angelo.' When she says that, I believe her at once. So, too, she says of Helena in *All's Well that Ends Well*, excusing her for her forwardness: 'She may be reckoned as one of the few women who have ever proposed for men and yet kept their charm.' I give in at once and believe her again. Or when she says flatly, of Claudio in *Much Ado*, 'Claudio is impossible', I feel that there is no more to be said. There is a passage in one of her sketches in which she imagines herself a man, and wonders which of Shakespeare's heroines she could have been happiest with:

I sometimes pass them all in review, wondering which I should have chosen had fortune given me a choice . . . Beatrice frightens me a little, but when I think of her at the other end of my dinner-table —Browning, Lord Leighton, and Mr. Gladstone listening delightedly to her remarks—I am a proud and happy man. Rosalind would be perfection for a week in the New Forest at Easter. Portia would mean exile. One cannot imagine her out of Belmont; but she would be a charming *winter* wife.

This is a fragment of the spirit which I desire to see. I must not omit to acknowledge Miss Agnes Mure Mackenzie's book of 1924 on the Women of Shakespeare: interesting, if Freudian: and more especially the delightful four lectures on Shakespeare by Miss Ellen Terry—first published in 1932, though composed soon after the beginning of this century. Two of the lectures are on Shakespeare's Heroines, and one would say that she had lived and talked with them.

I have ventured to regret that women have written so little about Shakespeare, and I can promise them a great reception from us men if they will only put on paper what they really think about the men and women of Shakespeare. They have a wide field to choose from, and there is only one of all these thirty-six plays which I should warn them to avoid, the only play of Shakespeare's, I think, in which they could not possibly succeed: I mean *Henry IV*, or the drama of Falstaff. I have always myself regarded this play as Shakespeare's recompense to men for his treatment of them in the comedies. In the comedies, as we saw, it is always the ladies who win, and I think we are agreed that they deserve their victory. But it is an easy victory; for the young men are never quite natural, which is as much as to say that they are never at their best. Can it be—I advance the suggestion in all timidity—can it be that women are at their best in the mixed society of men and women, and that men are at their best in the society of men? There is a passage on this matter in one of the letters of Keats. He had felt acutely this difference of feminine and male society, and had wondered at it:

Is it not extraordinary? he says. When among men, I have no evil thoughts, no malice, no spleen. I feel free to speak or be silent. I can listen, and from every one I can learn. My hands are in my pockets. I am free from all suspicion, and comfortable.

Every man who reads this understands what Keats means. Here is something in the art of living—an atmosphere of ease, of tolerance, of humorous equality, and of lazy good-nature—which women, with all their gifts, have perhaps not yet achieved. This humorous masculine club-room atmosphere Shakespeare has fixed for ever in the immortal scenes of Falstaff. It is the great secret of the comedy of *Henry IV* that it is wholly masculine and unaffected by women. The only women in those scenes are Doll Tearsheet and Dame Quickly, and you can see at once what informality this gives. One feels that when Shakespeare's ladies have retired, when they have quite left the neighbourhood, Shakespeare's men are so much—I will not say happier, because that would be discourteous, but so much more themselves. They unbend, and take their ease. An air of masculine undress descends upon them. They give up wit, and take to humour.

I am tempted to suggest, like so many men, that humour, this kind of humour, is not a feminine thing; but you will observe that I have not succumbed to the temptation. At any rate it seldom flourishes where men and women are together, except by some special licence of friendship or family or age. Cheerful abuse of each other is the principal delight of Falstaff and his friends; and I have authority for saying that this is wholly unfeminine. I say things to my friends, and my friends say things to me, which I am assured would end all friendship between two women. I believe that no fat lady ever lived who would take it like Falstaff. His friends exhaust the English language to find expressions for his shape, and the more they exert themselves the more he loves them. Remember Bardolph. He also had a physical infirmity which he is never allowed to forget, and it was among the principal minor pleasures of Falstaff's life to find adequate comparisons for this radiant feature—from the glow-worm in the dark to a ship's lantern in the poop. It might have been thought that the death of Falstaff would be a relief to Bardolph, thus consistently insulted by his master. On the contrary, there is no one more deeply grieved. When the news is told to him, 'Would I were with him', he cries, 'wheresome'er he is, either in heaven or in hell!' This is magnificent; and I am disposed to believe that it is masculine also.

Let the ladies, then, when they write those books which we expect from them, avoid the company of Falstaff and leave him to us. I believe it will be no great hardship to them; for I have seldom found a woman who really much cared for Falstaff, or liked his humour. To most women he will continue, I am afraid, to be a gross and corpulent old man, in whom men, from some masculine coarseness of taste, take a strange and immoderate delight. You may call these scenes of *Henry IV* the 'smoking-room' of Shakespeare's drama: a little corner of the house where men can relax and be merely men.

And yet, even here, the mocking laughter of women disturbs our calculations. Even upon Sir John the women of Shakespeare have their fated victory after all. There is *Henry IV*; but there is also *The Merry Wives of Windsor*. In an evil hour the fat knight turns lover; and in an instant his primacy is gone. He should have stayed in the smoking-room. The women fool him all the time; and he passes out, among titters and giggling, in a buckbasket, among dirty linen. *The Merry Wives*, we are told, was written at Queen Elizabeth's command, and I can well believe it. It was the most feminist proceeding of her reign.

What, then, to conclude, is the secret of Shakespeare's comedies: of their lasting beauty and power? It is no mystery. Their secret is the secret of Boccaccio's *Decameron.* As it has been said of that book, it is 'the secret of light and air'. A brilliant sunshine inundates and glorifies them. The spirit that inspires them is an absolute humanity unashamed and unafraid. You may sometimes be shocked by the language of your company; you may be shocked, but you will never be cold-shouldered. You may sometimes be incommoded by the diversity of your experience: but you are never melancholy, and you are never outcast. The World, which is the foundation of sanity, is always with you or near you. The World is made of Life and Hope: the Shakespearian Comedy is a portrait of the World. Boccaccio has been called 'the escape from Dante'. What is Shakespeare the 'escape from'? Shall I be accused of professional cynicism if I suggest that he is possibly the escape from his critics? Some of our modern analysts think that Shakespeare, in his comedies, might have gone deeper. The direction of his comedies, as of Boccaccio's stories, is rather to width than depth: but what is wrong with width? 'The world *is* wide, and its width supplies a kind of profundity in another dimension.'

III

THE DISLIKE OF COMEDY

I MUST ask you to face the odd and uncomfortable fact that there are people who do not like Comedy, who even *dislike* and fear it. In so serious a world what room is there for levity? What time is there? In a world so full of urgent problems (and you will have observed, no doubt, that nearly all public problems are urgent, that few are ever solved, and that nevertheless we go on)—but seriously, in a world so very problematic, how *can* this public jesting be right? When virtue goes so threadbare, is one justified in assisting at this organized gale of public laughter?

It might be thought that a sufficient answer to such gloomy questions would be a text of at any rate the comedies of Shakespeare. And so, perhaps, it would. But the protest is quite serious, and Shakespeare's comedies are suspect with the rest. There are people, for example, even in England, where Humour is understood, who have never forgiven Shakespeare for making his working people, and especially his crowds of working people, so gloriously absurd.

The persons who make this protest against Comedy are, as I am in the habit of dividing them, commonly of two classes. They are either Officials, and I use the word in the widest possible sense, representatives of institutions or vested interests; or they are Sentimentalists, Idealists, Enthusiasts for a cause. In other words, they have either something to conceal (and these are the Officials), or they have something to promote (and these are the Enthusiasts): and they are both uncomfortably aware that it is precisely from these two classes that Comedy draws her plumpest victims. Both types are familiar; you have, no doubt, your own examples. As someone said—he was a Cambridge man, and had made a study of their faces—'God has put that mark upon them so that we may know them'. You will find them all in Shakespeare. Dogberry and Polonius—the Policeman and the Cabinet Minister—will do for the Officials. For the rest—the variegated tribe of Sentimentalists and Utopians—the counterfeit Idealists—if you will allow a little for the change of fashions, you will find them in almost every one of the comedies.

If the things complained of were confined to the comedies so styled, I fancy there would be less grumbling. After all, it might be said, what *is* a comedy but an organized joke? But turn where you will in the drama of Shakespeare, the spirit of Comedy is seldom far off. It presents, in a play from English history, Jack Cade, the English Communist and Labour Leader, putting down, in a very foolish and ridiculous manner, Grand Dukes and education. In plays from Roman history—in *Coriolanus* and *Julius Caesar*—it insults (we are told) the democracy of Rome, and therefore democracy in general; and makes a laughing stock of Roman tribunes, the ancestors of all our Labour M.P.s Everywhere and always, so we are informed, it flouts and scorns the working man. Take Gravediggers. What is wrong with Gravediggers? Why, in the tragedy of *Hamlet*, should they be treated as clowns? They are only decent workmen doing their job. And why should the Porter in *Macbeth*—a member of a notoriously sober class—be represented in his one public appearance as drunk?

It is difficult to deal with this sort of criticism; and perhaps you may think that it is not worth dealing with. I used to think so. But this tense and touchy party has more people on its side than you would readily suppose, and some eminent names too: the poet Shelley, for example—and Shelley, with all his glaring and unworldly deficiencies, is not a witness to be ignored. Shelley, from the highest motives, had a profound prejudice against theatres, and especially against Comedy. His friend Peacock took him in hand.

I induced him one evening to accompany me to a representation of *The School for Scandal*. When, after the scenes which exhibited Charles Surface in his jollity, the scene returned, in the Fourth Act, to Joseph's library, Shelley said to me, 'I see the purpose of this comedy. It is to associate virtue with bottles and glasses, and villainy with books.' I had great difficulty to make him stay to the end. He often talked of the withering and perverting spirit of Comedy. I do not think he ever went to another.

Here we have a known man, and a man of the greatest genius. I make a great concession to the sentimentalist when I take him as a representative of their views. Is it blasphemy to suggest that Shelley's hatred of Comedy was, like theirs, a limitation of his nature, and due not to altruism entirely, but also to an instinct of self-protection? Few men of genius have done, or said, in their youth, with so terrible a gravity, so many ridiculous things as Shelley. Take this sentence, well known, I dare say, from one of his letters—a passionately serious letter to his friend Hogg. 'Is suicide wrong? I slept with a loaded pistol and some poison last night, but did not die.' May one laugh? Are not these sentences a gift to Comedy? Peacock *did* laugh, and accepted the gift, as you may see if you will read his *Nightmare Abbey*. It is a parody of a little clique of sentimentalists, men and women, with whom Shelley at one time lived—just such a sentimental segregation as Shakespeare, in his day, so loved exposing. Shelley appears as Scythrop: a young man troubled with the passion for reforming the world, and author of a treatise entitled *Philosophical Gas, or a Project for a General Illumination of the Human Mind*; nor is the pistol forgotten. There are few better scenes in English Comedy than the scene of young Scythrop, seated over a pistol and a pint of port, faced with the decision to take his life at 25 minutes past 7, and using the pistol to persuade the butler that the clock is fast.

Was Peacock brutal? Is this 'the withering and perverting spirit of comedy'? It exposes the folly of a young man of genius most desperately, but, in the eyes of Comedy, most ludicrously, serious about the state of his soul and the future of mankind. Has anything suffered? Do we think less of poetry and genius and of devotion to a great cause? Must we bite our lips, and refuse to smile at Shelley the preposterous undergraduate—Shelley the ludicrously solemn young reformer—reforming a world almost totally unknown to him except from books—and those books ill-chosen—Shelley the vegetarian, the ever-possible suicide, the pacer of churchyards, the hopelessly inadequate student of women? I think we *may* smile; I think we *ought* to smile; I believe we *do* smile, and that our admiration for what was true and lasting in him is unaffected—for his admirable unworldliness and his gift of song.

I return to Shakespeare and repeat: Does anything really suffer by the laughter of his comedies—anything, I mean, which we value? Do we think less highly of virtue, or of love, or of friendship, or of truth, or of simplicity, on account of it? Is it ever cruel? I think almost none of these things is true—any more than the modern charge of undemocracy often made against Shakespeare because in his picture of the common people of England and of Rome, he followed his authorities and his experience. The historians recorded that in certain risings and excitements the people and their leaders behaved foolishly, and Shakespeare, from this hint, makes them talk like fools. But with what tolerance! With what humorous affection! I know nothing more truly democratic in literature than the huge laughter of Shakespeare's citizen-mobs, and their goodhearted groping after the honest thing.

IV

SHAKESPEARE THE ENGLISHMAN

SHAKESPEARE to-day is not only an English but an international author; and no doubt the international importance of England has contributed to make him so. But this, as you are well aware, is a very small part of the explanation. The things of the spirit do not work in that way. It is by no means the largest or most powerful nations that necessarily produce the finest writers. Literature, thank God, depends on other things than population, and money, and guns. It is more than three hundred years since Shakespeare lived, and the England he lived in was a small and scattered nation: a nation of some five or six million people, whom he studied and loved and laughed at, after the manner of Englishmen. For it is a way of the English to laugh at themselves a little, now and then, for the good of their souls; to make jests about the things they would die for next minute, such as their country, or their regiment, or their countrymen and countrywomen, and all the things they love best. Why? I suppose, from some sense of decency and proportion, lest, like some nations known in history, they should fall into the sins of exaggeration and pomposity, and the madness of self-love. Shakespeare has been much studied in the last hundred years both on the continent of Europe and in America. You might pave the city of London with the books that have been written about him, and some will be left over. The authors of these books have been many of them learned men, and their work has its value; but you cannot read ten pages in most of them without discovering that they have never even begun to learn the principal lesson which Shakespeare has to teach. It is a lesson of the Comic Spirit; a lesson of humour and tolerance and understanding; of seeing two sides, and not taking oneself or other people too seriously. Ask any Englishman—and this is a matter on which Englishmen have a right to be heard—ask him and he will tell you that whoever has missed this lesson has missed, in his opinion, the main secret of Shakespeare. For Shakespeare, though his appeal is universal, is English to the core. Anyone who reads and understands him understands England: and not only the strength of England, but all its weaknesses as well. Shakespeare, like most Englishmen, suspected logic, and respected compromise: not from intellectual timidity, as some extremists assert, but from a profound conviction of the complexity of human nature and of all human affairs: life, he knew, cannot possibly be as simple as logic would make it. He was for balance, and order, and good-nature all round, and was at all times, and in all his works, the enemy of anarchy: for anarchy, he knew well, was the enemy of Freedom. I say Freedom rather than Liberty, because it better expresses Shakespeare's ideal. There is a great difference. Liberty is Latin and republican; Freedom is Northern and of the people. Liberty means the right of any citizen to call his neighbour in question, and complete Liberty therefore the right of everybody whatsoever to interfere with the concerns of everybody else. But Freedom means the right not to be interfered with—that Northern and very English right of being left alone. To all the fanatics of Liberty Shakespeare says, in effect, and he says it for England: if I want you I will ring. Shall a man not take his ease in his inn? Perhaps the best word for it is Tolerance, the *lesson book* of humour; and it is a good word to end with. I could wish we had a little more of it.

V

SHAKESPEARE'S PERIODS

BEFORE I approach the consideration of some of Shakespeare's early comedies and of the conventions in which they so evidently work, may I clear a piece of ground, and make some sort of perspective? Shakespeare was about twenty-six years old when he wrote his first play, and by the time he was thirty-six—from about 1590, say, to 1600—had composed some twenty plays in all (roughly two a year): histories and comedies mostly, with the spirit of Comedy still gallantly prevailing. A busy time, with all his acting and producing as well; but one must think a happy time, the private discord of the Sonnets notwithstanding. It is from that decade that we first hear of his candid good-nature, his facility in composition, his 'comic ease', as the phrase went, and his pleasant gifts as a companion. Another ten or eleven years of writing lay before him, years of still greater and very different achievement, during much of which his natural vein of Comedy was not absent, but in abeyance. The tradition of his personal character remained, however, unaffected. He was 'sweet Mr. Shakespeare', and 'gentle Mr. Shakespeare' to the end.

And that, I think, was right. I wish to protest, not angrily (that itself would be un-Shakespearian) against a tendency, which has long prevailed, to view all his work, and even the man himself, in the light of his tragedies—to make the writing of *Hamlet* in some undefined sense the goal of that astonishing first decade of his art, and the fact of *Hamlet*, and of the great tragedies which followed it, the master key to his life. I should have thought his *Midsummer Night's Dream*, *Twelfth Night*, *As You Like It*, the scenes of Eastcheap, are as absolute, or perfect, as unstinted in their kind as the later *Hamlet* and *Macbeth* in theirs, and as expressive of an inextinguishable part of Shakespeare's nature. You know what has happened in this matter. To trace the progress and development of Shakespeare's mind during his more than twenty years of play-writing has been, for over a century now, one of the principal scholarly occupations of Europe—and, for the last half-century, of America as well; nor is there any sign that his students grow tired. If England falters America takes it up; and all the while (at any rate until recent years) the *Gelehrten*, the trained bores of Germany, looking neither to right nor to left, and never never out of the window, ply, or plied, their pens for the Leipzig market. The results of these labours have been gradually stereotyped; and every child, for more than a generation now, has been able to inform itself by rote of the Periods, as they are called, into which the life and work of Shakespeare infallibly divide. Picturesque names have been given to these divisions: I am thinking more particularly of the late Professor Dowden's very useful little *Shakespeare Primer*, which has had so many imitators, and so few rivals: a masterpiece of too efficient vulgarization. The Periods, it seems, are four, and each has had assigned to it its own romantic name:

(1) First, In the Workshop: indicating those five years or so of Shakespeare's earlier career (1590–5) when he was learning his trade.

(2) On the Heights is the next: symbolizing (for the next five years) Shakespeare's rise to the summits of his craft.

(3) In the Depths is the third in order (1600–9)—though here there was some difference of opinion: another school preferring to vary the metaphor and say, In the Furnace—meaning, both of them, what is commonly called his 'Tragic Period'.

(4) And last, the period of Romance or Repose. You may choose which: for whichever you choose, you are to picture

a still handsome, if elderly, man, after all these oscillations—these singeings and burnings—writing, with a tired smile upon his lips, and a balance at the bank, somewhere about the years 1610 or 1611, *A Winter's Tale* and *The Tempest*.

I don't know what you think of this method. I should have thought, myself, that Shakespeare was pretty constantly in the workshop all his life—writing something like thirty-six plays in twenty years, and acting in so many more; and 'On the Heights', too, if we must use these Alpine metaphors. I would seriously suggest, also, that being 'On the Heights' is not a bad way of seeing into 'the Depths': that it is not necessary to suppose that Shakespeare had himself been in the Pit, because, from his unusual altitude, he saw so clearly into it. Still less do I appreciate the picture of amiable senility to which, we are told, we owe *The Tempest*. 'He had come through the Furnace', says the text-book, 'and had stood the test.' Or, referring to the romance of otherworldliness and ideal love which is so charming in *The Tempest* and *A Winter's Tale*: 'As he grew in years, his mind naturally reverted to the themes of his early manhood, and cast over them a sunset glow.' I appeal to you. Shakespeare, when he wrote these plays—the last in his career—was forty-six years old: and even if you think we are entitled to talk of a man of forty-six in this way, I ask you to recall the men of forty-six you know. Or, better still, go up to one of them and tell him your idea. Mention it to your tutor: it is possible that he or she may have actually reached this age, and still be obstinately clinging to office. Say that you suppose that, at such a time of life, minds naturally revert, and dwell with fondness on the themes of their early youth. I ask no other reward than to be told what answer you get.

We must be very wary how we apply such labels, such demarcations, to so mobile a thing as the life and work of a man. Shakespeare's mind had a history, and his art had a history: neither of them straightforward, or probably clear to himself: but at any rate a moving history, not to be thus confined. I welcome a remark of Mr. A. W. Pollard made ten years ago: 'One of the impressions about Shakespeare which have been strongly forced on me, especially of late, is that he was all of one piece. He developed, but in his development he cast nothing away. His attitude towards life deepened, but his outlook remained the same.' I agree: and refuse therefore to be browbeaten by this Tragic Period business, or to accept for a moment the portraits lately fashionable, and suggested by it, of Shakespeare as a moody neurotic genius, fallen away in those twelve years from all the traditions of his nature and the English cheerfulness of his youth. To speak of a master key of any kind to Shakespeare is probably presumption; but if a key must be found, at any rate to Shakespeare's daily life, I find it preferably in his comedies. So, I am glad to observe, does a profounder Shakespearian than myself, the analyst, still unapproached, of Shakespearian tragedy, Mr. A. C. Bradley. He puts a question. After all this talk about Shakespeare's supposed unhappy time, which of his plays, do you think, contains—not necessarily the fullest picture of his mind—but the truest expression of his nature, of his habitual daily temper? Mr. Bradley chooses *As You Like It*. I wonder if you agree.

VI

THE WORLD OF THE COMEDIES

THERE are two groups of characters in Shakespeare's comedies:

(1) The young men and women, who dwell in that romantically devised world, of youth, and dreams, and laughter, of which he possessed, and retains, the secret; and

(2) The workaday people, who keep things going—ploughmen, shepherds, servingmen, stewards, waiting-maids—with the unconverted drinkers, jesters, rogues, and odd fellows in a kind of limbo between the two regions—between upstairs and down—all plodding, stepping, tripping, and staggering along in a world of the four elements—of food and drink and sleep and labour. You may study this double world in any of these comedies: very fruitfully in *Much Ado* and *As You Like It*: most clearly, perhaps, in *Twelfth Night.* Like all these romantic comedies *Twelfth Night* is partly serious, and partly comic: a mixture of love and fun. The love story is the plot: it is serious, southern, and poetical. The comic story is the under-plot. It is not at all serious; it is anything but southern; and it is in prose. We don't at first know where we *are* when the play opens, and we very soon understand that it doesn't in the least matter. We are in the Utopia of lovers, where there is much despair, but no broken hearts.

All these plays are sweet with music: it is a part of this fairyland, the food of love. The Young Duke, being then in perfect health, sitting among his equally healthy lords, breathes out his luxurious agonies to the God of Love. It is a picture of eternal youth, framed in a setting of music, and poetry, and cushions, and flowers. What then, is the *climate* of these sweet tortures? Do we care? Viola comes to land.

> *Viola.* What country, friends, is this?
> *Captain.* This is Illyria, lady.

We are on those Adriatic coasts where the East and West lie so neighbourly—in Illyria—one of the Elysiums of fiction—and to most of us even now—as to almost all Elizabethans—not much more real than Ruritania. We hear in a distant sort of way of Candy and Crete, and ships named the *Tiger* and the *Phoenix*; and of a place called Messaline, which by some trifling oversight of Nature seems never to have existed. It has been searched for (though you will hardly believe it) by scholars, and rechristened Metelin, for Mitylene—because, I suppose, Mitylene is a real place. As if that mattered! This game has rules: and really, as visitors, we must allow the dramatist to pour out his own tea, and pull his own curtains!

I receive almost annually, from America and Germany, printed attempts to discover the 'source', as it is called, of *The Tempest*, and to locate Prospero's island in the Mediterranean or the Atlantic. The authors of these investigations are gentlemen for whom Utopias were not intended. There is an entrance fee to this club of good Utopians, which they cannot pay; of which they do not even understand the currency. Their children (who, by the way, get in for nothing)—their children could teach them better. Because, if you think of it, to imagine, even if it could be shown to be true, that anything is gained by knowing that Prospero's island was Lampedusa, and lay between Malta and the African coast—or that it was Corcyra, as another critic is equally prepared to prove—is to declare the play, on the whole, a failure. If the Island does not convince us, and convince us without any argument, that it lies precisely nowhere, it has missed its purpose, and the ideal impression which the dramatist was all along attempting to make upon us has not been made. The island has neither latitude nor longitude, because Shakespeare gave it none: and this will still be true, even if the moles should triumph: if the lost story which Shakespeare read should be unearthed; and some paltry original island be produced with a name and a place on the map.

Being an *idle* world, this world of romantic Comedy of which I am speaking: there are therefore students in it—but no lectures. There are a number of university students in Shakespeare: it was one of the choices of Elizabethan youth:

> Some to the wars, to try their fortunes there:
> Some to discover islands far away
> Some to the studious Universities.

Young Walter Raleigh was so thorough an Elizabethan that he had done all three—fought, sailed, and studied—before he was twenty. The most notable of all the young students in Shakespeare, and, one would guess, by far the most studious, is Hamlet; but he is outside our range. The Prince and his friends in *Love's Labour's Lost* are nearer our mark; or that bright spark Lucentio in *The Taming of the Shrew*. Lucentio was a graduate of the University of Rheims, and is supposed by his confiding relations to have entered on a post-graduate course at the University of Padua. I regret to say that there is no evidence that he even matriculated there, or, if he matriculated, that he ever did any work: unless you call it work disguising himself as a language-master, and teaching Bianca to misconstrue Ovid. 'Where left we last', says Bianca, coolly.

Luc. Here, madam:
Hic ibat Simois; hic est Sigeia tellus;
Hic steterat Priami regia celsa senis.
Bian. Construe them.
Luc. *Hic ibat*, as I told you before, *Simois*, I am Lucentio, *hic est*, son unto Vincentio of Pisa, *Sigeia tellus*, disguised thus to get your love; *Hic steterat*, and that Lucentio that comes a wooing, *Priami*, is my man Tranio, *regia*, bearing my port, *celsa senis*, that we might beguile the old pantaloon.

A young puppy, you see!

Bian. Now let me see if I can construe it: *Hic ibat Simois*, I know you not, *hic est Sigeia tellus*, I trust you not; *Hic steterat Priami*, take heed he hear us not, *regia*, presume not; *celsa senis*, despair not.

A nice pair! As Grumio says in the same play: 'See, to beguile the old folks, how the young folks put their heads together!' It has been the same since Menander. Lucentio's father, we are told, had his misgivings about his son, and they were not ill-founded. But the young man takes risks for love, and Shakespeare, therefore, sees him through.

In this climate of Romance, it is, of course, the rule that all the lovers shall love at once, and love absolutely. Nothing else, in this world, is to be permitted. One glance at Olivia, and no work need be expected from Orsino for some time to come. Olivia herself, *grande dame* though she is, succumbs in one interview: they are all struck from heaven. Only two of these couples have the temerity to stand off for a time, and assume, at any rate, the postures of defence—I mean Rosalind and Biron, and Benedick and Beatrice—and there are special reasons for that. This Utopian Love is what the Elizabethans called *Fancy*: bred neither in the head nor in the heart, but in the eyes. We call it 'love at first sight'—and, really, I have never heard that it wears worse than any other. The eyes are not the *least* intelligent agents either of the head or of the heart. It has, of course, some disadvantages, this remorseless way of loving, from the point of view of the performers: (1) it must be acknowledged to be extremely open to ridicule; (2) if everybody did it, there would be an end of all society. The trouble is, that true love alone can never make a comedy. True love is serious, and Comedy should amuse. It is exclusive—most terribly so—and Comedy should be friendly. It is unsocial—it cannot be hidden from you how very unsocial two lovers can be!—but the subject of Comedy is Society. Comedy is a plump figure, and holds its sides; Love is lean, and holds a hand upon its heart.

What is to be done? Is *Romantic* Comedy, then, impossible? Must either the laughers or the sighers be given up? But which? *Not* the laughers, surely! Does true Comedy mean no more cakes and ale? Shall there be no Comedy but

Mr. Shaw's? But then—a play *all* laughter? What is to be done?

Shakespeare proceeded, as he always does, by compromise. If Comedy laughs, Romance is not to be offended; if Love sighs, Comedy promises to put up with it—to a point! to a point! If the jokes are good, and the sighs are true, there would appear, on this undertaking, to be no reason in literature why they should quarrel. In Romantic Comedy, therefore, the laughers and the sighers live side by side, like good neighbours: on only *one* condition: that neither shall commit excess, or compete for attention at the expense of the other. And this is sound. For what is more wearisome than the uninterrupted spectacle of lovemaking in which we have no share? Or more awful than the gravity which falls upon a company that has laughed too much, or giggled too intellectually? The law, therefore, is one of decency and measure. The solemnity of Love is relieved by the generosity of Laughter, and the irresponsibility of Laughter by the seriousness of Love. This is the principle of Romantic Comedy, and for a compromise—how admirably it works! No one ever managed it so well as Shakespeare. The words of Mercury need not be harsh after the songs of Apollo.

I don't know a better or more convincing demonstration of this compact than to pass from Orsino and Viola in the first two scenes of *Twelfth Night* to Sir Toby and Maria in the third—from Illyria to the Buttery Hatch. The first two scenes pitch their language high. Romance is to be secured on her throne before Comedy comes in. Olivia being in mourning for her brother's death, Orsino has sent a messenger with kind inquiries. Maria very properly refuses to admit him, and informs him that her mistress does not intend either to put off mourning or go into society for seven years. This is how Valentine reports to Orsino:

> So please my lord, I might not be admitted;
> But from her handmaid do return this answer:

> The element itself, till seven years' heat,
> Shall not behold her face at ample view;
> But, like a cloistress, she will veiled walk,
> And water once a day her chamber round
> With eye-offending brine; all this, to season
> A brother's dead love, which she would keep fresh
> And lasting in her sad remembrance.

I am quite sure this is not how Maria said it, or anybody but an actor. The style goes on. Since Viola has escaped drowning herself, there is a hope that her brother may have escaped also, especially as the Captain saw him tied to a mast. This is how it is put:

> Mine own escape unfoldeth to my hope,
> Whereto thy speech serves for authority,
> The like of him.

These are phrases neither of men nor of angels: only actors ever spoke them. Viola and the Captain now walk off: a door seems to open: we step into the Buttery: and a voice cries 'What a plague means my niece to take the death of her brother thus? I am sure care's an enemy to life.' With what a comfortable sense of shock we encounter this underworld. This is the very tune of unconverted man, and every ear is ready for it. It is the dialect of life. The etiquette of Romance is exacting: how pleasant it is to step downstairs! How snug it is. A different syntax controls the speech of these quarters. The air seems to change. It is Illyrian no longer. These strayed revellers, fools, and drinkers, who raise the owl at midnight, and burn sack to bring in the morning (because it is too late to go to bed), and talk of Puritans and weavers, and count the bells of St. Bennet—one, two, three—were never bred on the Adriatic. Every member of the audience, and every reader, knows that he is at home again —in the paradise of humorists and odd fellows—in England—among friends. The blood of the living Falstaff is in Sir

Toby Belch; Sir Andrew might have sat on the same bench with Justice Silence; and Feste, the third man and best singer in the trio, is no other than Will Kempe, fool-in-ordinary to the company of the Chamberlain's Servants.

This was well understood by Shakespeare's audience: there was a tacit understanding at that time between the audience and the stage that the entrance of the comic characters indicated a temporary suspension of the romantic or historical fiction on which the serious action was based; that the assumption of a strange country or a different period of history had been dropped. This is the practical explanation of several liberties in more serious plays and even in Tragedies. Such was the Porter in *Macbeth*, with his jokes about Garnett the Jesuit and last year's harvest. No one supposed him to be a porter of ancient Scotland. Here was a primitive convention which Shakespeare maintained.

It is in his power over these two worlds, in his ostensible alternations between Nowhere and England, that Shakespeare's romantic comedies excel all others.

VII

SHAKESPEARE'S WOMEN

LECTURES on Shakespeare's women have become, as the wits of our time remind us, something of a provincial pastime, a standing dish for the suburbs: and, no doubt, the thing has been overdone. But I have no choice in the matter. Of all the angles of approach to Shakespearian Comedy, the master angle is, and must be, the angle of femininity.

A certain clear-headedness, a frankness in facing facts, a power of deciding what is to be done, are the peculiar and distinguishing marks of Shakespeare's happy women. When they are by themselves, these young ladies, or with a friend, softness will steal in. A kind of languor descends upon them, like the weariness of a hostess when all her guests are gone. They remember that they are women; that women's hearts are waxen; that 'such as they are made of, such they be'. Sometimes, for a moment, they break down altogether. But in public, their courage never fails them. With every pang of affection and anxiety they only grow more witty. They even exult in their peculiar power of being cool and decisive in exact proportion to the strength of their passion and the sentimentality of their men. There have been men—critics —who objected to these heroines of Shakespeare on this very ground. It used to be an opinion of men—and there are some survivors from the masculine shipwreck of our times who believe it still—that most women are by nature sentimental, and designed by Providence to be clingers upon men. All women, probably, agree with Shakespeare. He does them more honour. He pays them the high compliment of supposing that they may have knowledge, shrewdness, wit, and courage without ceasing to be wholly feminine and the objects of desire. In his ideal woman the heart and head sway equal. Beside her, man, especially if he be in love (as it is ten to one the poor fellow is), man is a creature of extravagance, all head one moment, all heart the next.

> For, boy, however we do praise ourselves,
> Our fancies are more giddy and unfirm,
> More longing, wavering, sooner lost and worn,
> Than women's are.

So speaks Orsino in the comedy of *Twelfth Night*, and he speaks for Shakespeare. In woman alone, Shakespeare seems to say—not in all women, by no means, but in the best—will you find that perfect harmony and balance of the parts of human nature, which is the basis and first condition of a happy life.

I used to point out to my students, years ago, how odd it was, and how characteristic of most of Shakespeare's young women, that we hear so little of their parents, and so especially little of their mothers. I thought that I had been the first to notice it. But I had been forestalled by Miss Ellen Terry. It is true, anyhow. Not many of them seem to have a mother; and partly, no doubt, this is a stage convention, because, when love is in the air, mothers are only in the way. Convention or not, Shakespeare liked it and meant it. One notorious exception there is, in *Romeo and Juliet*; and, as everyone has remarked, it makes a world of difference to our feeling for Juliet's tragedy that she is still a mere girl, with a mother still thinking for her and her old nurse still waiting on her, when she rushes into the sudden maturity of her passion for Romeo. Had she been left, like most of Shakespeare's young women, to take care of herself, he would have been sure to ask for a little more of the discretion of this world.

It is an amusing, though illogical and perhaps blasphemous, game to *plant* mothers in these plays, and guess what happens. If Desdemona had had a mother, it is likely (though a mother, writing to *The Times*, has denied this) that Othello would have been a much less frequent visitor at her father's house in Venice, and that Desdemona would have made a more normal marriage. Of Miranda with a mother it is not easy to think; for the whole idea of this heroine is founded on her never having known a mother. Not only Miranda, but Prospero and the whole island change into absurdity at the terrible entrance of Madame Prospero. A magician with a wife is not an easy conception, and Prospero *en maisonnette* suggests too violently the Swiss Family Robinson, with Caliban for the native servant.

The Rosalinds, Portias, and Beatrices, of course, need no mothers, nor do they seem to desire them. They appear, indeed, to have very little use for parents of either sort. Most of them have fathers, who are preferred to mothers by Shakespeare and other dramatists, because, I suppose, they are less in the way. It is one of the advantages of a father, from this point of view, that he is out so much. Sometimes he is passed over even when he exists. There is Julia, in *The Two Gentlemen of Verona*; and we should have expected her to be more considerate. That she has a father we learn only from her maid. 'Madam' (she says), 'dinner is ready and your father stays.' This is all we ever hear of that elderly gentleman: that he was once kept waiting for his dinner. When Julia decides to leave home in disguise, one might have thought that she would at any rate leave a message for the old man. Not at all. His name is never mentioned. 'All that is mine', she says to her maid,

> All that is mine I leave at thy dispose,
> My goods, my lands, my reputation.

Julia escapes by ignoring her father, but Rosalind, Orlando's sweetheart, is franker. When she meets her exiled father, the Duke, in the Forest of Arden (and of course he doesn't know her, because of her boy's clothes), does she rush into his arms, like the distressed daughter of later days, and weep out her story on his shoulder? She does not. 'I met the Duke yesterday', she remarks to her friend Celia, 'and had much question with him. He asked me of what parentage I was; I told him, of as good as he; so he laughed and let me go. But what talk we of fathers, when there is such a man as Orlando?'

So, too, Helena in *All's Well That Ends Well.*

> O, were that all! I think not on my father,
> And these great tears grace his remembrance more
> Than those I shed for him. What was he like?
> I have forgot him. My imagination
> Carries no favour in it but Bertram's.

Whatever parents may think as they shake their heads over the younger generation—and when have they not done so? —there is no doubt that Rosalind and Helena were right.

Shakespeare, of course, has not confined himself, even in his comedies, to this one type of heroine, though it is clear that this is the type of woman he preferred. He has drawn the softer, the more conventional type as well. Julia, in *The Two Gentleman of Verona*, in spite of the treatment of her father, is such a type. She is one of a small, a very small, number of women in Shakespeare who may be called sentimental. And what happen to her? What you might expect in Shakespeare's world. Julia, the sentimental, clinging Julia, who satisfies every convention for a young woman in love, is abandoned by her lover; while Sylvia, who takes her own way, who is perfectly independent and clear-headed, and refuses to be bothered by the silliness of men, suffers not from a want of sweethearts but from too many—the most persistent of them being, in fact, the very gentleman who had deserted Julia. There are others like Julia, of whom Mariana in *Measure for Measure* is the most glaring example, and they have all the same fate. Cling as they may, and satisfy every convention, they cannot keep their lovers or command success.

What are we to infer? Anything? If anything, certainly this: that to succeed in life and in love, in the world as Shakespeare saw it, a woman must have wits, and brain, and spirit, as well as heart. In the cases I have named, since they are from his comedies, there was no incurable disaster. By means however careless the spirit of Comedy patches up some kind of happiness for them in the end. But look for a moment at the tragedies of Shakespeare, where this genial spirit of Comedy gives no help. Observe what happens to the conventional heroine there. Ophelia, in the tragedy of *Hamlet*, in many respects, is such a heroine; and so also, I say it with hesitation, in some respects, though not in all, is the tragic young wife of Othello. We all pity Ophelia, and she deserves our pity. Perhaps it is all she asks. She is one of the tragic failures in Shakespeare's world, a world in which success in life is not given to the merely innocent and loving. I do not forget—it would be unforgivable to forget—the share which Fate has in the disasters of Ophelia, and of Desdemona; but it is clear enough why Shakespeare drew them as he did. They, and particularly Ophelia, are victims to inexpressiveness. They have lived, as sentimental women do, in a world of dumb ideas and feelings. They have never skirmished and pelted wit with men like the bolder and happier women of the comedies. To say that they are less worldly than the Rosalinds and Portias is hardly the truth. They have been saved from the world. They have never had to defend themselves in sport, and they are unable to defend themselves when it comes to earnest. They cannot even realize —which is the most pathetic thing of all—that it *is* earnest.

Much has been written, in England and elsewhere, on the divine purity, humility, and innocence of these tragic heroines, and, no doubt, their fate is heart-breaking. But they are no purer, no more innocent, nor in any true sense more humble than the witty, loving, laughing, faithful, happy women of the comedies. They are tragic, not from any quality which they possess too good for this world. Such a quality does not exist. They are tragic, so far as they have responsibility for their fates—they are tragic from defect: because they want, what the Rosalinds have got, clear heads and ready tongues as well as loving hearts, the gift to be happy and make others happy. They can do everything but understand. In ordinary life, I imagine, they were the kind of women whom Shakespeare least liked to meet. They impede the world, these women, clinging about its neck, so that it depends upon the mood of the world, and not upon themselves, whether their end shall be tragic or not. Shakespeare felt for them, and if their end was tragic, pitied them, and made them pitiful to us. But the women he admired and most delighted to portray were the women who carried their destinies with them, and in speaking and thinking as well as in feeling were the equals and superiors of men. Miss Ellen Terry appreciated them.

I must make Beatrice more *flashing* at first, and *softer* afterwards. She must be always *merry* and by turns scornful, tormenting, vexed, self-communing, absent, melting, teasing, brilliant, indignant, *sad-merry*, thoughtful, withering, gentle, humorous, and gay, Gay, *Gay!* Protecting (to Hero), motherly, very intellectual—a gallant creature and complete in mind and feature.

There is Silvia, again, in *The Two Gentlemen of Verona*. She is just going to bed when music is heard in the garden, and up through the air floats this masculine account of her.

> Who is Silvia? what is she?
>   That all our swains commend her?
> Holy, fair, and wise is she;
>   The heaven such grace did lend her,
> That she might admired be.
>
> Is she kind as she is fair?
>   For beauty lives with kindness:

Love doth to her eyes repair,
  To help him of his blindness;
And, being help'd, inhabits there.

Then to Silvia let us sing,
  That Silvia is excelling;
She excels each mortal thing
  Upon the dull earth dwelling;
To her let us garlands bring.

There are one or two small objections sometimes made to Shakespeare's comedies which perhaps I ought to mention—especially as they are made, not by enemies of Comedy, but by Shakespeare's friends. Of the thin jesting and quibbling and light bawdry, I say nothing now: that flaw, for flaw it is, can be dealt with later. But it is sometimes complained that Shakespeare in his comedies is careless of his women: that having first made them attractive, he gives some of them, in the end, very doubtful husbands. Well, there is no doubt something in it. Proteus and Julia, Oliver and Celia, Claudio and Hero, Bertram and Helena, Angelo and Mariana: it is impossible to be happy about such alliances as these, or to think that the dramatist was very fastidious when he made them. But we must not ask too much. Every dramatist in this matter is to be regarded as an embarrassed parent with a bevy of marriageable daughters—proud to have arranged some good matches, and particularly that especially suitable one for the Beauty of the family—but heartily glad to have them all settled somehow: to have them, as we say, 'off his hands'.

There is another complaint sometimes made, though not so often of late, for a reason that will be plain to every reader of the modern novel. It used to be objected that all these affairs in the comedies of Shakespeare end precisely at the point where affairs become interesting: in other words, at marriage. First courtships, at the date I speak of—not so very long ago—were thought a little threadbare. The moves, it was hinted, were too obvious and the players were too young. How much more interesting Rosalind and her Orlando would be—not, as we see them, skirmishing in their teens, but experienced, thirty, in slippers, with 'those little lines' beginning to gather about the mouth—and, shall we say, a dinner not too well cooked. I am afraid that, quite apart from excellent theatrical considerations, Shakespeare took the reactionary view, which was the view of his time, that when the Priest had said the words, the Great Adventure was over: the rest was household politics, and politics, he knew, made bad plays. Happy marriages have no annals of which plays can be made; and unhappy marriages did not seem to him, on the whole, a subject for Comedy. He makes only one exception: if the lady is a shrew, and must be taught her business a rousing comedy it shall be. But if things go wrong—really wrong? If this happens, Shakespeare may be counted on. He makes a Tragedy of it; and that house is cleansed by earthquake. Always, in this matter, Shakespeare is drastic and clean-minded. There is no doubt much jesting on the weaker side of marriage; jealousies flare up, and very scandalous charges are made. But of no play of Shakespeare's can it be truly said that Infidelity is its subject; the successful rake and the really doubtful wife are absent from his gallery.

VIII

SHAKESPEARE'S CLOWNS

ONE must suppose that there have always been Clowns. We appear to need them, and therefore they are born. There is a moment, when we have all had our say about the world, and sufficiently tired each other with our wisdom, when it is felt that the fool should be heard. Folly is free; it can say what it likes; and brings messages sometimes from strange territory: that half-explored tract or no man's land, where sense and nonsense fraternize. In the Holbein picture of Sir Thomas More's family (as Dr. Johnson, rather unusually, notes) the only servant represented is Pattenson, his fool. This is a proof, the Doctor remarks, of the familiarity to which fools were admitted, not by the great only, but the wise. He might have added, as one of many proofs of the sagacity and humour of Sir Thomas More, that fools, professional fools, are expressly provided for in his *Utopia.*

There are roughly two types of them: one, half wit, half natural; the other, part fool, part knave. Each type has its varieties, and an astonishing number of these varieties are to be found in Shakespeare.

He seems, this sort of stated fool, to have begun in villages —like almost everything else good and lasting in English life. The rustic fool, the bumpkin, is the father of all the rest. He first appears on the stage of life somewhat vacuously chewing a straw. Later on, the more promising specimens of the class are taken, as we say, into gentlemen's service; given a uniform and board-wages, and made subordinate officers of households. Our ancestors, in the days of little reading and few visitors, looked round for relaxation, and set up the domestic fool. By the fifteenth century he had become an established institution. Edward IV's fool, John Scogan, was still remembered in Elizabeth's time, and *Scogan's Jests* was a popular book of Shakespeare's boyhood. King Henry VIII had his fool, the famous Will Sommer, whom Wolsey hated so for his pointed comments on pampered favourites. All through the sixteenth century court fools appear in the accounts of the Royal Household, and the fashion was continued by the Stuarts. The last famous court fools in England were Archie Armstrong, whom King James brought with him from Scotland, and his successor, Muckle John, in the time of King Charles I. After the Restoration the professional fool, so far as I know, ceased to exist at the English Court, though a few specimens lingered on in noble houses in this island even into the nineteenth century. Sir Walter Scott reports that, even in the eighteenth century, the Earls of Strathmore had a family fool with a holiday dress of full motley with bells of silver, and that as late as 1800, in the house of one of the first noblemen in Scotland, a jester of this kind stood at the side-table during dinner, and amused the guests with his presumably impromptu quips and sallies. I have myself heard, as a boy in Scotland, and read also, in chapbook form, some of the sayings of the family fool of a nineteenth-century Laird of Udny in Aberdeenshire.

What substitutes we have found for this long-established institution I am not quite clear. The evening newspaper, the music hall, the wireless, cover some of the ground. Perhaps the nearest thing to it in the life of a modern household is the practice known as 'having in the children'. The innocent shrewdness and *naïveté* of the questions and answers of children may at least suggest to us what our fool-keeping ancestors felt the need of—in the days (those far-off days, as they now seem) when children might be seen, not heard. In the East, of course, the household fool is ancient, and he still goes on. The impulsive gentleman, who was till lately King Amanullah of Afghanistan, maintained, with no sense of incongruity, at once a private broadcasting station and a court jester.

On the stage I suppose there have always been Fools or Clowns. Certainly every popular stage has always insisted on some clowning. The people is not averse to solemnity; *likes* it indeed; and will accept with almost gruesome alacrity the most solemn and the most harrowing themes. But it has always asked that there shall be a laugh *somewhere*—even if the play should happen to be about the Bible and the Fall and Redemption of Man. The old Miracles had always their bright patches of comedy: a handy sheep-stealer, with the sheep hidden in the cradle, or some potent and homely figure like Noah's wife. Also, if Deity must be spared, then Devilry must bounce for it, and be amusing; so that Satan and his Vices became comic characters in England. It was in the reign of Elizabeth that the old Vice went out on the regular English stage, and Mr. Clown, as we know him in Shakespeare, came in. If you are curious about origins you might glance at a play called *Misogonus*, in Mr. Bond's collection of *Early Plays from the Italian*. You will there see the domestic fool just entering on his short but very distinguished dramatic career. By Shakespeare's time he has acquired his technique, and practises it in amity with a host of companions less exalted than himself in the profession of folly. It was Tarleton —Richard Tarleton—who achieved the double role for which English comedy had been waiting, by becoming at once the official jester of Queen Elizabeth's court and the star Clown upon the London stage. Tarleton's is a name to be mentioned with respect. He created a part and a tradition; and Dan Leno and George Robey are among the direct descendants of his art. He was discovered in the country, somewhere in Shropshire—keeping his father's swine. A servant of the Earl of Leicester fell in with him; was struck with his *happy unhappy* answers; and brought him as a find to court. The court could never afterwards wholly part with him, or London either.

The best short account I know of the Elizabethan clown is in the second volume of *Shakespeare's England.* You will there find the institutional background of Shakespeare's Clowns; and you will see a picture of the great master of Elizabethan clowning—Dick Tarleton himself. He is worth looking at: a stocky sturdy figure (for it was a vigorous trade), in what is apparently a russet short coat and trousers, with low shoes (*well strapped*, observe, for like all good clowns he was an expert dancer, and much given to standing on the toe), with a drum hanging from his belt, and a tabor from his lips (for clowns must also be musicians)—a drumstick in the right hand, his left hand fingering the pipe—and what I take to be a money-box (it looks a little like a beer jug, and a little like a water-bottle) hanging from his belt: for tips. Clowns expected to be tipped, and sixpence was not too much, as you may learn from Shakespeare. Costard, in *Love's Labour's Lost*, makes it plain that three farthings were not enough, even if you called it, not a tip, but 'remuneration'. A little further on you will see another picture of a professional clown with the long coat which was the traditional dress of the idiot; the half-wit; the *born* fool. It was no doubt patched with the motley: red and yellow. This figure carries no instruments at the moment; but he has not forgotten his long purse. Turn another few pages and you will find a stage picture of the Simpleton: eating, apparently, a large slab of bread or cake. I gaze on it with respectful wonder—with the emotions which more responsible minds experience when they regard the first model of the steam-engine or the spinning-jenny: for it is the lineal ancestor of Harry Lauder's Scone.

The two extremes of clowning were the rustic fool and the court jester. All the varieties are mixtures of these two. Their task was, of course, the general one of making the company or the audience laugh, and, more particularly, of keeping the dialogue going in the intervals of action. They supplied also, when necessary, both *Song* and *Dance*. Even

Dull the constable joins the general break-down at the end of *Love's Labour's Lost*. In the exchange of conversation, their technique, their principal and expected contribution—as you may see from any comedy of Shakespeare—was (consciously or unconsciously) to extract fun from words. It was a foible of the age, which Shakespeare thoroughly and unaffectedly shared, to be everlastingly excited and amused over the forms, shapes, sounds, and meanings of words: and a foible easy to understand, for the language was bubbling over with new inventions. Much licence was allowed; and when the fool is proficient, he never lacks partners among the ladies and gentlemen. It is a brisk bandy-ball of words, and we tire of it before they do.

It was the fashion of the time to call these comic persons all, indifferently, Clowns: but obviously there are great differences. I think the best division of the professional comic men in Shakespeare's plays—at any rate, the best division technically—would be this: (1) those who play with words; and (2) those who are played with by them—those, that is, who are sufficiently masters of the English language to make fun out of it; and those who are so mastered by it as to give fun unconsciously. I don't know what you think: but with one or two exceptions—Touchstone perhaps, at his best—I find the second, the helpless class, more amusing, and of a more lasting humour, than the first.

(1) In the first class come all the professional Fools, headed by Touchstone, with Feste, and such court-bred attendants as Moth—that 'tender juvenal'. In the same class, though touching on the second, come the men-servants, the roguish valets, like Speed, and Launce, and Launcelot. They see the fun well enough, but, sometimes, through illiterate ambition, they take a fall.

(2) In the second class come rustics like Costard, artisans like Bottom, and officials like Dogberry, Verges, and Dull. The amusement they cause is at their own expense. They are

complacent, vain, and adorably stupid. Sometimes they achieve pure nonsense, than which nothing is more difficult to explain. Margaret Cavendish was right. Somebody, in Charles II's time, had been complaining that Shakespeare's Comedies are made up of clowns, fools, watchmen, and the like. And if it is so, she replies, what more difficult (or when done, more satisfying) than these same comic characters? 'For 'tis harder to express nonsense than sense, and ordinary conversation than that which is unusual.' I agree with the Duchess. There is nothing in Shakespeare more certainly the work of genius than the *mettled* nonsense, the *complacent* nonsense, the perfectly contented and ideal inanity which Shakespeare, in some of these characters, has presented to us. Dogberry the head-constable—a person of some importance—who is sure that Borachio will be 'condemned to everlasting redemption'; who bids his company of the watch 'comprehend all vagrom men' and 'aspicious persons'; who believes that 'comparisons are odorous' and thinks a good many things 'most tolerable and not to be endured'; this, it has always been felt, is a considerable personage; but how much richer than even this Dogberry is the better, the less ambitious Dogberry, quietly and simply stating his mind in the language which God has given him.

Goodman Verges, sir, speaks a little off the matter: an old man, sir, and his wits are not so blunt, as, God help, I would desire they were; but, in faith, honest as the skin between his brows. . . . A good old man, sir; he will be talking: as they say, 'When the age is in, the wit is out'. God help us! it is a world to see. Well said, i' faith, neighbour Verges. Well! God's a good man. . . . An honest soul, i' faith, sir; by my troth he is, as ever broke bread: but God is to be worshipped: all men are not alike; alas! good neighbour.
Leonata. Indeed, neighbour, he comes too short of you.
Dogb. Gifts that God gives!

Dogberry is unveiled. It is a profound and awful revelation of the official mind. I descend from these heights to lower and shallower ground. What are we to say of most of the verbal combats of the comedies, when the Fool leads? Of the stale puns—half a scene in the *Two Gentlemen of Verona*, for example, turning on the jingle between 'ship' and 'sheep' —then pronounced alike, and pronounced alike still in the west country? Of the continual forced mismeanings and intentional misunderstandings, that a poor jest may be born? Of the same old jokes and pranks perpetually recurring: Biron, Dogberry, and Falstaff all telling us, in three separate plays, that Pitch is Pitch, and will defile? Of the eternal horn and cuckold jest, in which *all* indulge, both men and women? the assurance, in every play, that some people have more hair than wit: which is no doubt true, but tedious: the jokes about diseases, and *such* diseases: all that stock-in-trade of the Clowning Game; what are we to say about it?

(1) That it was once alive, certainly; but equally certainly that most of it is now dead and must be written off. It was local and temporary always; and if you pluck it, it dies. (2) Further, that we are not now dealing with a purely dramatic question: but very largely with a stage question, in which the audience also was involved. It was not a new question, even in Shakespeare's time. This kind of jesting is very ancient, and has always gone on when the dramatist is compliant, and the audience immature. Plautus did it for the ancient Romans as Shakespeare does it for the Elizabethan English, and Molière, sometimes, for the French: and all for the same reason. The type is heavy with age.

An unsophisticated audience—and after a good dinner any audience—loves this sort of thing—still loves it—but to-day, as it happens, we are in a position to discriminate. We send such things to a music hall, to variety—where I for one will always promise to enjoy it. In Shakespeare's time the problem was not so simple. These distinctions between one theatre and another had not yet been made. From one and the same stage, and from every play acted on it, all delights were hoped for, from the greatest to the least, from the grossest to the most delicate. If in the same act you could both tickle the palates of the audience and poke them in the ribs, or make them shiver one moment and grin the next, you were the dramatist for their money.

Shakespeare, more than any of his eminent contemporaries, complied with this taste. He was generously affable and careless about such things, and the stage manager of the Globe had no reason to regret his affability. He was an actor, and he wrote for all parts of the house. His plays are strewn with jokes to the gallery—some of them those good old jokes that go on for ever—about Growing Bald (on which he could joke feelingly), or about Policemen (such policemen as they had —the Dogberrys of the age), or about Henpecked Husbands, or Stewed Prunes. The great Mother-in-Law joke had not yet been invented; if it had he would undoubtedly have made great use of it.

Shakespeare in time, of course, paid for all this and lost a little from the next generation of what he had gained by humouring his own. The day came, and came quickly, when the weaker jests of his Clowns were despised. The new wits of the Caroline age, the new men of the town, found them stale, *vieux jeu*. There are some well-known partisan verses about it by William Cartwright and John Birkenhead, writers themselves, and admirers of the new firm of Beaumont and Fletcher, Shakespeare's younger successors. You may read them among the prefatory poems to the 1647 edition of Beaumont and Fletcher's works.

> Shakespeare to thee was dull whose best jest lyes
> I' the Ladies questions, and the Fooles replyes;
> Old fashion'd wit, which walkt from town to town,
> In turn'd Hose, which our fathers call'd the Clown;
> Whose wit our nice times would obsceanness call,
> And which made bawdry pass for comicall.

Birkenhead echoes Cartwright, and actually finds excuses for Shakespeare, as for a primitive:

Shakespeare was early up, and went so drest
As for those dawning hours he knew was best;
And when the Sun shone forth, *You Two* thought fit
To wear just Robes, and leave off Trunk-hose wit.

'Trunk-hose wit', as we might say 'Victorian', 'Crinoline', or 'Antimacassar' wit. It is baldly expressed, and it was written for a purpose. If you wished to praise a dramatist to the skies, you said that in some things he had improved on Shakespeare. But there is a dash of justice in it: which we may admit the more readily when we observe that it does not, and did not even then, diminish the sovereignty of Shakespeare's comic genius. Even the keenest admirers of Beaumont and Fletcher praised Falstaff, and quoted him eternally, as the finest comic character in the world. It was the Clowns, the set fools, they thought little of: and this was not so much a censure of Shakespeare as of the Elizabethan stage and the Elizabethan public: to which, however, it was thought Shakespeare had been too lenient.

The Clown was at this time so much a stock character that he is sometimes not even given a name; and he relied so much on 'gagging' that in his entrances he is not even given a part: 'Enter Clown, say something, *exit*.' He was a stage rather than a literary property, and his secret is contained in a single name: the name of Tarleton. Richard Tarleton the comic actor created the part of the Clown, and created it so effectively—so completely captured the age—that writers of comedy had to provide him with a part whether they wished to or not. As a rule, I should think, they were only too willing: for Tarleton was of that class of comedian who has only to walk on and look at the audience, to throw it into screams of laughter. There was nobody like him, and all London mourned when he died. He is Spenser's Pleasant Willy, and probably Shakespeare's Yorick. Tarleton died in 1588, before any of Shakespeare's work appeared on the stage; but he left successors who continued his tradition. He was succeeded by Will Kempe, his understudy. Kempe had a great reputation as early as 1589, which lasted until his death in 1609: and he was no sooner dead than his place was taken by another student of Tarletonizing—Robert Armin. Armin was at his height in 1610, and was supreme in his own line during the earlier half of James's reign. It is a complete succession for more than a generation. Kempe was Shakespeare's man. He was the original Dogberry in *Much Ado* and Peter in *Romeo and Juliet*; he probably acted Launcelot, Launce, Touchstone, Feste, and the Gravedigger in *Hamlet*, and, generally, took the Clown's part as a matter of course.

We are apt to think of the dramatist as all-powerful in these matters. But it is not so now; and it was not so then. Indeed the balance was quite the other way. Like the later Harlequins, these professional Clowns 'claimed the limited licence which *x* enjoys in mathematics'. The Tarletons of the stage prided themselves on being able to do without the dramatist altogether. Tarleton and Kempe were celebrated for what was called 'extemporal wit'. They made things up as they went along. They gagged, and we have it on record that these were often the most taking parts of their performance. The better dramatists bitterly resented this tyranny of the comic actor—see Shakespeare's injunction in *Hamlet* to say nothing but what was set down for them, aimed at Kempe. In time the best of them revolted against it; but for the most part, if they wished to be popular, they had in some degree to submit. Shakespeare submitted with a better grace than most. Also, remember:

(1) That the part of the Clown in Shakespeare was not written *in vacuo*: it was written with one eye on Kempe. It followed, therefore, to some extent, Kempe's methods, and Kempe's type of joke. Shakespeare may even have learned something from Kempe, as Molière did from Scaramouche.

(2) The other comic parts, though they might differ from the stock part of the Clown, were inevitably infected by it:

for this reason, if for no other, that their performers were obliged to play up to the Clown, and as the phrase went 'minister occasion' to him. Even here, therefore, the art of Tarleton and of Kempe must have guided the hand of Shakespeare. If I am not exaggerating, this explains a good deal; and should not be forgotten when we remark on the sameness of some of the jests in the comedies, and the strong family likeness there is in much of the routine work of the Clowns themselves. To us, a great part of this fooling is only half alive. Punning, to begin with, has long been out of fashion; and in any case, the quibbles in these plays are either not clear to us, or they are threadbare. We know them too well, or we have to read a commentary to see the joke: a test which few jokes survive.

The other element, that of mistakes and genuine misadventures with words, has more life in it to-day. The language was then churning with new formations, mostly from the Latin, and the evidence is riotous that the Elizabethans delighted in them. They might condemn other people's Latinisms, but they rejoiced and languished over their own. This is a taste which will probably never go out. We have still Town Councillors and Mayors and Tribunes of the People who try to make their language climb to the height of their great vocation. Launce's 'prodigious son'; 'the merry days of desolation' that Costard had seen; poor Dull's 'allusion', 'collusion', 'pollusion'; the rich fruitage of Dogberry and Mrs. Quickly: this Malapropism is never dead. 'Comparisons are odorous' to Dogberry, you remember, and rascals, by the same dignitary, are 'condemned to everlasting redemption', their lives being 'most tolerable and not to be endured'. The thing goes on. The excellent Yorkshire woman is still alive, the delight of her employers, who uttered in my hearing these impressive words of pure Dogberryism: 'There', she said pointing, 'There goes a nutritious scoundrel'!

We laugh at the mishaps of Dogberry and his friends, and we were meant to laugh. He was a willing victim of the age. I wish to remind you, however, that Dogberryism—old Dogberry and all his house—and there is one in every village—have been, and still are, a great force in the unlearned colloquial life of England. For inquire: what happens to Dogberryisms: what is done with them? They are by no means lost. The unlearned take them up and find work for them.

IX

THE TEMPEST

I

It is a matter of some interest to playwrights that the first notions or rudiments of *The Tempest*, of all his plays the least local and circumstantial, should have been drawn by Shakespeare from a contemporary event. The enchanted island, the storm, the wreck, the miraculous preservation, and the sad meeting of the diminished fleet—these, the recognizable first elements of the play, by a process which, when we speak of Shakespeare, we feebly call magic, were imported by the dramatist from life. It was in the summer of 1609 that this tempest rose and fell, driving the Admiral ship of the Virginia fleet with all hands on the Bermudas. Nearly a year passed, and they had long been given up for dead, when the whole party, Admiral and all, appeared one day in two vessels of their own building on the coast of Virginia. They had had a miraculous escape, 'not a soul perished'; and had emerged from the perils of an island which was, they declared, most certainly enchanted and the home of devils.

They returned to England, where they were received with much wonder and thankfulness, and their strange narrative was eagerly read. It was read by Shakespeare, who instantly perceived the possibilities of an adventure so richly compounded of Providence, magic, and the sea. 'His mind and hand went together.' Last autumn's tale was still fresh in men's minds when in 1611 *The Tempest* was finished, and down for performance before the king. In these matters, it would appear, there are no rules, but only genius and happy casualty.

The story of the play is distinct from these foundations, and less important; nor is its origin yet known. It would almost seem, indeed, as if Fortune had here resolved to punish the presumptuous curiosity of scholars. She has certainly played them a teasing game. Twice, if report be true, the original has been found, printed in choice Italian; and twice, through helplessness, it has been lost again. The first to find it was the poet Collins, the author of the *Odes*. 'I was informed by the late Mr. Collins of Chichester', says Thomas Warton the historian, 'that Shakespeare's *Tempest*, for which no origin is yet assigned, was formed on a romance called *Aurelio and Isabella*, printed in Italian, Spanish, French, and English, in 1588. But though this information has not proved true on examination, an useful conclusion may be drawn from .it that Shakespeare's story is somewhere to be found in an Italian novel, at least that the story preceded Shakespeare. Mr. Collins had searched this subject with no less fidelity than judgement and industry; but his memory failing in his last calamitous indisposition, he probably gave me the name of one novel for another.' This is probably the truth. The last years of Collins's brief life were clouded by insanity. But the 'friend' who told James Boswell, the son of the biographer, that 'some years ago' he had 'actually perused an Italian novel which answered to Mr. Collins's description', had no such excuse. The trouble, it may be supposed, was this, that both Collins and Boswell's friend were amateurs; the detection of sources was not their trade. If one of the professional editors had had their good fortune, if Theobald or Steevens or Malone had stumbled on the story, it would be known to-day in a dozen reprints. As it is, the story is still to find; and the chance of its being found seems more remote than ever since a scholar of the last century, bent on redressing the tricks of chance, explored his way through every Italian novel before Shakespeare without lighting on a trace of what had twice been lost. Some day, no doubt, the original will be discovered. Meanwhile, those of us who are inclined to set a lower value on these originals than their discoverers are apt to do, may with great patience await the day.

Baffled in their attempts to discover an original, the critics and antiquaries have not therefore despaired. The names of the characters have engaged their interest. Where do they come from? Like most collections of names, from all quarters. There are a Prospero and a Stephano in Ben Jonson's *Every Man in His Humour*, in which Shakespeare had acted. From this play, it has even been asserted, Shakespeare learned the pronunciation of Stephano, which is always right in *The Tempest*, 'Is not this Stephano, my drunken butler?', and always wrong in *The Merchant of Venice*, 'My friend Stephano, signify, I pray you'. Of some other and more interesting names—Caliban and Sycorax and Setebos—the pedigree is less easy. The only explanation of Caliban that I remember to have seen is the old explanation of Dr. Farmer. He believed, and Malone agreed with him, that the name was suggested to Shakespeare by the title of that chapter in Florio's Montaigne, 'Of the Canniballes', which we know him to have been reading when he sketched Gonzalo's commonwealth in the second act. By transposing the letters of the word 'Canibal', the name 'Caliban' may be formed. A modern reader is little likely to be impressed by such an explanation; but it must be allowed that the twisting of words, of proper names especially, into anagrams in this way was a universal foible of the age, so that to do it well ranked as one of the minor accomplishments of a gentleman.

Of the other outlandish names, only Setebos has been tracked to its source; for the explanations of Sycorax (Psychorrhax=ψυχορρήξ=heartbreaker, *et hoc genus omne*) are monuments of desperate conjecture. Setebos has proved a more fruitful quarry. Some one pointed out that the name of the chief god of the Patagonians was Setebos, and Dr. Farmer, following the hint, found it at last in Eden's *History of Travel*. That Shakespeare knew this book, which was a book of his time, that he had read the passage in which the powers of this god are described, and taken the name from it, was likely in itself. But it became certain when Malone made the further discovery that Eden's *History* contains, besides the name Setebos, the names of five of the characters in the play. Alonzo, Ferdinand, Sebastian, Gonzales, and Antonio all figure in its pages.

This is an astonishing instance of what may be found by dogging an author's footsteps. There was no reason in the world why Shakespeare should go to Eden or any other writer to find such names as these. They are common Italian or Spanish names, open to every one. But it has been often remarked how dependent the most inventive writers are on happy accident for the names of their characters; and surely no man ever went about the business of collecting items for a play with more appearance of indifference than Shakespeare. He is as casual in his borrowings as his own Autolycus. He does not search, but unconsidered trifles come in his way. When the play is started, and the characters on foot, it is a different matter; he is everywhere at once with them, like a spirit of air to whom distance is a dream. But in the beginning of his journey he travels light, like one who knows the roads and can be sure of his inn.

II

The most trying thing in playwriting is to make a beginning. When the dramatist sets out, his invention is not yet warm. He desires to be in motion, but shrinks involuntarily from the strain. When this feeling is overcome and his conceptions begin to stir, he is met by a fresh difficulty, not peculiar to his art: the necessity to be explicit without being dull. There are things to be explained before the play can go on. The audience must know the facts; and the facts must be communicated, willingly or unwillingly, in some sort of narrative, which is a thing of all others the most abhorrent to the stage. Shakespeare, like all good dramatists, disliked it heartily; and what is more, he seldom did it well. In many of his plays, in his English histories especially, he writes at the beginning dully and crabbedly, as if it were a task, what it was necessary for the audience to know. He not only disliked narration; it is to be suspected that he had by nature only a moderate interest in plots. His interest was in character and passion, in humour and fancy, and in the achievement by art of a certain total impression.

In *The Tempest* we are privileged to see the dramatist seriously at work upon this preliminary difficulty, and mastering it by such strokes of dramatic art as it is our business to disclose. The play opens with a storm at sea; and we are presented at once with its two first elements, of all elements the most romantic for a story, a wreck and an island. Shakespeare, within a period of three years, described three storms at sea: in *Pericles*, in *The Winter's Tale*, and in *The Tempest*. They were received, as such powerful descriptions must have been, with applause and delight; and as the greatest painters will repeat even with precision their finest effects, so Shakespeare has repeated his effects in these plays in the same strain of language, and sometimes even in the same words. Johnson thought the opening scene of *The Tempest* 'perhaps the first example of sailor's language exhibited on the stage'; but Johnson forgot *Pericles*. Those who doubt most the genuineness of *Pericles* are forced to grant that none but the author of *The Tempest* and *The Winter's Tale* could have written the storm scene in the third Act, where the dead wife of Pericles is sunk in the sea.

The storm in *The Tempest*, since it was the last to be described, has benefited by its predecessors; and in any case it means more in that play. In the two other plays, the storm, however calamitous, is an incident; in *The Tempest*, since the wreck is on a lonely island, the storm is everything. In

Pericles, therefore, we see it only from the deck; in *The Winter's Tale* only from the land; but in *The Tempest* from both. How striking to the senses the first scene of *The Tempest* can be, those who still remember their sensations when they first opened this play are best able to tell. There is no opening scene in Shakespeare comparable to it for suddenness and certainty, unless it be the meeting of the witches in *Macbeth*. In the life of the scene Shakespeare finds himself so much at home as to be in danger of outrunning his design. The boatswain begins to exceed his function and become a full-grown character.

> What cares these roarers for the name of king? . . .
> What, must our mouths be cold?

are lines not easily forgotten. We grow to love 'this wide-chapped rascal', who so perfectly commands the rights of things. Neither rank nor danger can deter him from his office; and while all are howling he is pithy to the end. Could the scene have lasted longer, had his place been anywhere but under hatches, we should not have had to wait for the end of the play to renew his acquaintance.

When the second scene opens we are on the island and in the thick of the storm once more, in Miranda's moving description; we learn further, from the first words she speaks that we are in the presence of its author. The masterly art of this long scene cannot be too much admired. The first part, 186 lines in all, is occupied by the dialogue between Prospero and Miranda. This dialogue serves various ends. It acquaints us with the past and gives the pulse of the present. Before it is finished we know Miranda and Prospero almost well enough to infer the rest of their behaviour. We can imagine Miranda's simplicity in love, and we become acquainted with Prospero in his two darling characters of magician and father. The majesty of the magician is softened by vanity, and the dignity of the revenger by kindness of heart. Early in the conversation he lays down his magician's mantle, and talking with as much simplicity as his habitual impressiveness will allow, he tells the history of his daughter's childhood and of their coming to the island.

> 'Tis time
> I should inform thee further. Lend thy hand,
> And pluck my magic garment from me.—So: [*Lays down his mantle.*
> Lie there, my art.—Wipe thou thine eyes; have comfort.

When the tale is told we know not only who they are, and how they came there, but also who were on the ship and why they have been wrecked. From the assurance that no harm has come to them, and that the moment approaches when Prospero's fortunes will be mended or marred for ever, we conjecture that the reappearance of our first acquaintances will not long be delayed, and that strange things are brewing.

A lengthy dialogue of this sort, unrelieved by interruption, must have been tedious and dull. The facts which it discloses could no longer be withheld from the audience, but there was a danger that the audience, as well as Miranda, might be charmed to sleep. The devices employed by Shakespeare to secure the movement and interruption necessary on the stage are so highly ingenious that they may be recounted in full. He interests the audience and interrupts the stillness of the actors by making Prospero vary his postures and busy himself about his clothes: by making him divest himself of his magic robe and wand when he sits down beside Miranda, and resume them again when he rises with an air of business near the end of the dialogue, and bids Miranda sit still to hear the close of his tale. The dialogue, also, is a real dialogue. It has no languors. Prospero cannot go fast enough for Miranda's questions, nor Miranda be attentive enough to satisfy Prospero. He breaks off his story six times to urge her to attention. All this has its effect on the audience. Miranda's excitement and her anxiety for further disclosures affect in equal proportions their curiosity and their goodness of heart. They feel that they are privileged to hear secrets; and they remember that she has no mother. The main purpose of Prospero's interruptions does not strike them: to the more discerning they discover only the magician's desire to see how his charm is working, and to the less discerning only an old man's testy habit. All are impressed, as the dialogue nears an end, by Prospero's impatience: clearly something important is about to happen.

The moment Miranda falls asleep Prospero turns to business and calls on Ariel to appear. Once more we hear of the horrors and amazements of the wreck. The account this time is literal, and is given with gusto; Ariel has no turn for sentiment, but like a good artist thinks first of his technique. It is not merely 'Enter Ariel'; it is 'Enter Ariel and all his quality':

be't to fly,
To swim, to dive into the fire, to ride
On the curl'd clouds:

he is instant and answerable for all.

Prospero Hast thou, spirit,
Perform'd to point the tempest that I bade thee?
Ariel. To every article.
I boarded the king's ship; now on the beak,
Now in the waist, the deck, in every cabin,
I flam'd amazement: sometime I'd divide
And burn in many places; on the topmast,
The yards, and bowsprit, would I flame distinctly,
Then meet, and join: Jove's lightnings, the precursors
O' the dreadful thunder-claps, more momentary
And sight-outrunning were not: the fire and cracks
Of sulphurous roaring the most mighty Neptune
Seem to besiege and make his bold waves tremble,
Yea, his dread trident shake.
Prospero. My brave spirit!

A high professional pride, very touchable by flattery, and a certain bright egoism of the air, shine through the punctilio of this perfect servant. Others, mere departmental spirits, might have caused these lights to burn; he was himself the flame.

> All but mariners
> Plunged in the foaming brine and quit the vessel,
> Then all a-fire with me. . . .

While he thus exuberates he never exceeds. Ride as he may on the spirit of his orders, not a letter is broken and to the greatest tests he brings the excitement of art. He is as exquisite in protection as in terrorism: far from suffering by their wetting, the garments of his victims are even 'fresher than before'. This bettering of his promise is attended by an admirable economy. The mariners might so easily have been made to leap overboard, like the rest, but how inefficient, since their place was under hatches. They therefore stay.

We are now deliberately assured of the safety of the ship and its inmates, and are prepared for the approaching entrance of Prince Ferdinand, already in his own sad fancy King of Naples. At this point, by what looks like chance, Ariel's good nature deserts him. He turns 'moody', and grumbles. There is thus contrived, by the simplest of strokes, an opportunity to insinuate without appearing to impart the further information which we desire. Prospero, in a fit of righteous anger which every employer of labour in the audience thinks just and natural, takes the liberty of recounting to the ungrateful Ariel his past history: the miseries of his former existence, his miraculous release, and the terms of his service.

While we learn so much we are prepared for more. By the account which we hear of Ariel's enemy, the witch, we are prepared for the most difficult entrance of all, the entrance of the monster Caliban. It was not, we may suppose, for fuel that Prospero chose this moment to visit the monster's cell.

Caliban's protest, 'There's wood enough within', may very well have been just. But it was essential, before going further, to complete our review of the inhabitants of the island, and exhibit the last extravagance of its domestic economy. Caliban, by a contrivance no longer new, is also 'moody'; so that we hear his history also, partly from himself in sullen recrimination, partly from his master Prospero in angry retort. Last of all, to conclude the scene, there enters to the sound of Ariel's music Ferdinand the Prince, so soon to be plain Ferdinand the lover. The detachment of Ferdinand from his companions, and his arrival at the cell, are the first moves in Prospero's game. He must have freedom to fall in love before his party appears. The natural simplicity of his first meeting with Miranda and of their charming conversation does not conceal, and was not meant to conceal, the outrageous match-making of the fond father, which cries out to us in every aside. The only persons ignorant of it are the lovers themselves; and this is as pleasing as it is true to life. Prospero is both father and mother to Miranda, and plays the full part.

If the scene has a fault, it is that it tells too much. There is a danger that the *dénouement* may be too plain. The rest of the play is almost wholly made up of minor designs and misadventures, which are only held together by Ariel's dispatch. On his celerity in executing orders everything depends. When the second act opens, Ferdinand being already in Prospero's hands, and the crew asleep under hatches, there remain to be disposed of two groups of persons: the king's party (which is a solemn affair), and Caliban's party (which is not), each with its conspiracy. The surveillance of these two groups is Ariel's task, and on the proper performance of it the play turns. Prospero had foreseen the conspiracy against Alonso's life, and sent Ariel, first to give it opportunity, and then to frustrate it. The other conspiracy, designed by Caliban, was Ariel's own discovery. 'This will I tell my master.' He enters at the very moment they make it, and with his voice from Nowhere sets them all by the ears. Into this employment Ariel throws himself with gusto and research; it is in a sense his own business, and he lays it on. His other task, the distracting of the shipwrecked nobles, he performs, indeed, 'to point', but never with relish, and in the end comes near to pitying them, though a spirit.

Prospero's interests were naturally different. He was interested most in his designs upon Alonso's party, which contained his usurping brother and his friend Gonzalo, and in his daughter's love-affair with the prince. So long as these went well, Prospero, who was no Napoleon, was apt to take his ease and let the world slide. In the fourth act he finds time to melt the magician in the father and carry out a promise he had made to exhibit to the young people 'some vanity of his art'. A masque of marriage blessing is hastily contrived; Ariel himself condescends to take the part of Ceres, and everything is going finely, when suddenly Prospero starts to his feet and in a kind of frenzy dismisses the pageant, which vanishes heavily with strange and confused noises. He had completely forgotten the other conspiracy, and at any moment Caliban and his confederates might break in! When he has apologized to Ferdinand, 'Bear with my weakness; my old brain is troubled': he calls instantly for Ariel, who puts his fears at rest. He had guessed that Prospero had forgotten, but like a good servant, observing his master's preoccupation with family matters, had said nothing about it. He had already, indeed, taken the affair into his own hands, and, as Prospero freely admits, had done his work on the wretched conspirators as thoroughly as man or magician could desire.

III

Now why, it may be asked, should the plot have been so complicated that Prospero himself could not hold the threads?

Why should the dramatist confuse the magician? Why have two conspiracies? Why have any? These are certainly questions to be asked. One motive for these conspiracies can hardly escape observation. Shakespeare wished to insinuate the inability of men to live together, in numbers however small, in places however remote, without intriguing against each other's lives and properties. But he had a further motive. The government of the island, it is to be observed, is a bureaucracy; and a bureaucratic government, from its very nature, is the deadly enemy of all drama in the public life of its subjects. The only way of alleviating the monotonous spectacle of lawless but absolute power, which such a government presents, is to incite its agents to infidelity and its subjects to conspiracy. Shakespeare, with unfailing insight, has provided both alleviations. He has made Prospero's agents moody and uncertain, and he has invented two conspiracies, one of them, at any rate, aimed at the very centre of power. It is not for nothing that Prospero breaks down in the fourth act, and repents of his art in the last. His sovereignty was not only in itself unlawful, as based on forbidden arts; it was also dangerous and insecure, as based on the collaboration of difficult and unwilling subject powers. Ariel grumbles, and is at last only persuaded to serve for two days more; Caliban declares that Prospero's spirits 'hate him rootedly'. The conviction that he is handling difficult forces, which only constant vigilance can restrain from desertion or treachery, gives a human interest to the magician's performances which they must otherwise have lacked. We are enabled to share his anxieties in the fourth act, and to echo his relief at the beginning of the fifth, when he finds his charms effective, his spirits obedient, and his enemies in his power.

But even when this had been done, more remained to do. It was not enough to show the flaws in Prospero's sovereignty; some exercise of freedom was necessary among the victims of his magic, if the balance of will was to be dramatically preserved. We know them to be puppets in Prospero's hands, and are content that it should be so; but if from first to last they shared our knowledge, we should find the spectacle of their contortions either intolerable or dull. To remove the difficulty Shakespeare contrived the two conspiracies, and to this end the first and less interesting conspiracy is more necessary than the second. The party of nobles among whom it occurs are almost continuously under the influence of enchantment, so that a display of free will is more needed among them than among the others. The party led by Caliban are allowed more control of their natural wits, because their wits and the free exercise of them are the only passports which Trinculo and Stephano possess to a place on the island.

These general motives are perhaps in themselves a sufficient justification of both conspiracies. Their more immediate and more obvious motives are part of the machinery of the play. Conspiracy by its nature removes disguises, and exhibits character under the rose; we know our men well before the end. This end, to which everything conducts, is simple. Like all finales it turns on time and place. It is the principal concern of Prospero's stage-management, from the second scene onwards, by every means that art can devise, and through such trials and discipline as may seem necessary, to bring all parties punctually to the same destination. The first step was taken when Ferdinand was detached. His companions have to pass through many troubles on their way; their minds have to be prepared, and their consciences awakened; but their route, thanks to Ariel's shepherding, never falters. Slowly but steadily, through all interruptions, they are led, they know not how, towards Prospero's cell. Of the common men of the party, none is allowed to land but Stephano and Trinculo; for when the sailors come in, with the boatswain at their head, everything is over but the blessing. Stephano and Trinculo, the drunken butler and the professional fool, are allowed to walk the island for the sake of their humours; and might have walked there without misfortune to the end, but for their fatal facility in listening to Caliban when he proposes the destruction of Prospero and the capture of the isle. The lust of empire seized them, and they were paid in cramps. Their humours, however, were at the bottom of it all. Had they not promised to be amusing, Shakespeare would not have troubled to make them conspirators. He wished to exhibit them to his audience; and in order to exhibit them without dispersing the action he had to attach them to the plot. Had they continued to be unconcerned in the issue of the play, Ariel's sport at their expense must have seemed irresponsible foolery, unworthy of one who measured work by seconds. As it was, their meddling relieved Ariel of the trouble of guiding them to the rendezvous. Prospero's cell was their deliberately selected destination, and Caliban led the way.

The forming of this conspiracy had a further consequence, obvious to every one, and of the first importance: it took Caliban from his faggoting and trencher-scraping, and brought him into action among men. To have allowed this strange, malignant, plaintive creature, all senses and peering mind, to remain hidden and unexercised throughout the play, could never have been contemplated by his creator, and would never have been forgiven by any reader of the second scene. In selecting Trinculo and Stephano to be his associates, Shakespeare showed as much philosophy as art. To exhibit primitive man in communion with the parasites of civilization has now become a profession, but was then novel and untried. The beginnings of religion and the rude origins of government are visible in his readiness, first to call them gods, and then to be their subject. As a satire on the grades of society these scenes may be compared with the system of *A Midsummer-Night's Dream.* Bottom looks down on the fairies as the butler and the jester look down on the monster; and they are all in their turn most justly and methodically looked down on by the lords and ladies who make the high life of these plays. Primitive man, it is to be observed, though easily deluded by sham, is quick to know reality when he sees it. Caliban early learns to despise Trinculo; he is on the point of despising Stephano, when the conspiracy is frustrated; and he sees the truth at last when his master appears among the reconciled nobles at the end of the play.

> I'll be wise hereafter,
> And seek for grace.

The Tempest is singular among Shakespeare's plays for the perfect regularity of its structure. All those rules of dramatic art (the unities of place, time, and action), which in his other plays he seems to take delight in breaking, are here exactly and even minutely observed. This is remarkable both on general and on particular grounds. It is remarkable that a dramatist who all his life had flouted the classical rules of drama should, in perhaps the last play he ever wrote, so strictly observe them. It is doubly remarkable when we remember that *The Tempest* is almost contemporary with *The Winter's Tale*; that within the limits of one year Shakespeare wrote the most regular and the most irregular of all his romantic plays. Every excess of which romantic drama is capable will be found in the construction of *The Winter's Tale*. It is as loose, rambling, and disorganized as *The Tempest* is knit, compact, and orderly; and this is the more astonishing since their subjects are so similar. In *The Winter's Tale* the scene changes from one country to another, characters are born and grow up in half the time of a performance, and the *dénouement* is not reached until the fourth act. In *The Tempest*, the scene of the action is as nearly as possible unchanged; the time of the action does not exceed by much more than an hour the time required to represent it; and the play, leaping all preliminaries, enacts the *dénouement* only of its plot. The difference of method is absolute.

How far this difference was the result of accident, how far of design, it is impossible to determine. Shakespeare may have wished to show the critics that he was as good a man with the fetters on as without them, and could obey their laws and break them with equal facility. Or the regularity of *The Tempest* may be an accidental effect of the story from which he drew. However we explain it, Shakespeare takes an evident pleasure in the unaccustomed speed and precision of movement. The action of the play, we are frequently reminded, is the work of a single afternoon. It begins about two by Prospero's hour-glass, and might be expected to end about six. This was Prospero's estimate in the second scene, and his confidence in Ariel's ability to keep within it was fully justified by the event. When the fifth act opens we learn from their conversation that the sixth hour is near, but not yet come. This insistence on the time of day is very noticeable. We can understand why Prospero, whose scheme depends on speed, and Ariel, who works by contract and does everything in seconds, keep so sharp an eye upon the hour-glass. But Shakespeare goes out of his way when he brings in Alonso and the boatswain in the last scene to confirm their reckoning. His design was to impress us with the swiftness of the action: with the rapidity of Ariel's transits and of Prospero's effects. We feel that not a moment has been wasted, and this feeling gives cleanness and adroitness to the finish.

The sensation of speed is assisted by the style. Every reader of Shakespeare who is alive to the effects of literary form must feel, at the very entrance to this play, the strange mastery of its speech. In some of the earlier scenes, with their packed sentences and breathless syntax, the rush of thought seems to ride down and trample underfoot the fixed forms of language. The laws of prosody share the same swift fate with the laws of syntax. He is triumphant over both. No irregularity is refused which may loosen the verse and make it fitter for dramatic use. Surplus syllables, not only at the end of the line (which is a common excess), but at any place within it; trisyllabic feet, which became so popular with the later dramatists for the sake of the trip that they give to the verse; and those final unaccented monosyllables weakly called 'weak endings', which are so impossible in rhyming verse and so convenient in the continuous blank verse of drama—all will be found scattered freely through the play. We are leagues removed from the earlier blank verse which ran so infallibly into couplets, and left the ear straining for the missing rhyme. The fault of this later verse is not that it stops when it should go on, but that it tends, in passages of excitement especially, not to stop at all. But where no great effort seemed to be required it has an air of masterly negligence, which imitates to perfection the rapid sinewy rhythm of dramatic speech. This way of writing verse did not come by chance. It was the late fruit of practice and maturity. Some parts of *Pericles* and *The Winter's Tale*—those other 'storm plays'—are written in this manner. It is a manner peculiarly open to corruption. *The Tempest* is one of the twenty plays which first appeared in the First Folio edition, and there is therefore no other authority for the text. This might well have been a matter for regret. But the truth is, the Folio text is so clear of imperfection that the absence of any other version is even a matter for congratulation. Where there is no problem, it is idle to amass evidence. The play reads as if it had come straight from Shakespeare's hand. It has difficulties, indeed, but they lie in the writing; they are due neither to editors nor to printers, but to the style of the author. No text in the whole of the First Folio better justifies the boast of its editors that they had printed plays from Shakespeare's own versions. 'His mind and hand', they tell us, 'went together: And what he thought, he uttered with that easinesse, that wee have scarse received from him a blot in his papers.' This ill-concealed brag has been terribly handled by our later men of method. But if any manuscripts of this sort did reach them, it is as certain as such things can be that a manuscript of *The Tempest* was among them. The temptation to make all smooth, to straighten a little the crooked syntax and amend a little the freedoms of metre, must otherwise have been too strong. The inference is that they were relieved of decision by a higher authority than usage. They had the author's own words before them.

IV

Any one who has read *The Tempest* simply for the sensation it gives to read fine poetry, and who has besides enjoyed the representation of it on the stage, knows very well that when we have described the construction of the play and the action of its characters there is a great deal that we have left unsaid. No English play ever written provides so well for the different needs of reader and audience. Character, humour, and poetry are open to both; but whereas a reader thinks himself well served with the poetry alone, an audience has everything besides that makes audiences happy; sweet music, fine shows and pageants, singing, and dancing. This was the dramatist's design. *The Tempest* was written for an audience, and was intended to satisfy to the utmost both the eye and the ear.

A reader may not much regret the shows and dancing; but to miss the music and the singing is to miss two things that, if they be well performed, are the very pulse of the play upon the stage. Music floats through it everywhere. Ariel can do nothing but to music: he sings 'Where the Bee sucks' while acting as valet to Prospero in the last scene. It is one of the subtleties of the isle: magic and music go hand in hand. It is even, as everyone has seen, a touchstone of character; we guess men's dispositions by what they say about it. We know Ferdinand as well by what he says of Ariel's music as by anything else that he either says or does.

> Where should this music be? i' th' air, or th' earth?
> It sounds no more;—and sure, it waits upon
> Some god o' th' island. Sitting on a bank,
> Weeping again the king my father's wrack,
> This music crept by me upon the waters,
> Allaying both their fury, and my passion,
> With its sweet air: thence I have follow'd it,—
> Or it hath drawn me rather.

This is the language of the childhood of nature, the language of a goodness which owes nothing to civilization but its names; and this goodness, by the same test and by this test only, we find in Caliban also, when, like a child, he tells his companions of the music of his dreams and his bitter tears. Nothing more betrays the depravity of Trinculo and Stephano than their insensibility to music. Ariel's music only scares them. Swabber songs are their line, and even in these they cannot keep a tune, but are corrected by Caliban, who is unable not to know a tune once heard. That Shakespeare believed in this test of music we know well from other plays than this. Trust not the man whom music cannot move, says Lorenzo, speaking more for Shakespeare than for himself: he has a treasonous mind. True to this judgement, the only man in King Alonso's party, who remarks on the sweetness of the music in the magic show, is the only man of the party who bears a clear conscience, the good Gonzalo. The conspirators say nothing.

The shows and pageants of the play mean little to a reader, and are generally run hastily over as dull. The speeches in such shows were rarely meant to move apart from the spectacle, though Shakespeare's are finer to read than most. But think what such spectacles meant, and still mean, to a natural, unjaded audience! Johnson knew this. 'The shows and bustle with which his plays abound', he writes in his Preface to

Shakespeare, 'have the same original. As knowledge advances, pleasure passes from the eye to the ear, but returns, as it declines, from the ear to the eye. Those to whom our author's labours were exhibited had more skill in pomps or processions than in poetical language. . . . He knew how he should most please.' These spectacles, in Shakespeare's day, were taken seriously. Audiences were critical, for many among them had taken part in pageants themselves. They were not to be put off with slovenly work; everything must be well done. The directions are explicit: 'Enter certain Reapers, *properly habited*'. Even in small matters—and yet it was not a small matter either to a stage-manager—this care to satisfy the eye of the audience may be observed. 'Go make thyself like a nymph o' the sea,' says Prospero to Ariel: 'Be subject To no sight but thine and mine; invisible To every eyeball else.' Why, asks the commentator, should Ariel do anything of the sort, since no one was to see him but Prospero and himself? The answer is, that the audience was to see him, and that he must match with the scene. The first part of *The Tempest* is full of the tones of the sea; and as a sea-nymph Ariel more fitly chants the invitation to the sprites to dance upon the beach, and the requiem over the sea-change of Ferdinand's father.

When we come, as we come now, to speak of the magic of *The Tempest*, we are at once sensible how difficult and almost impossible it is to separate the practical magic of the play from the ideal, the magic of Prospero from the magic of Shakespeare. The practical magic of the play is visibly and audibly in the charm-working music, the taboring, singing, and dancing; in the fading pageants and apparitions; and in the staring, awestruck eyes of the enchanted. The greater and higher magic is in the total impression of ideal habitation that Shakespeare gives; and the two can scarcely be disjoined. There is nothing in the practical magic of the play to contradict this ideal impression: nothing homely, like Puck and the company of Peaseblossoms in the magic of *A Midsummer-Night's Dream*; nothing earthy, local, or gross, like the witch-magic of *Macbeth*. 'We are sensible,' says Maurice Morgann, in his celebrated essay on *Sir John Falstaff* (1777), 'both of a local and temporary and of a universal magic. . . . Of the first sort the machinery in *Macbeth* is a very striking instance; a machinery which, however exquisite at the time, has already lost more than half its force; and the Gallery now laughs in some places where it ought to shudder. But the magic of *The Tempest* is lasting and universal.' The study of demonology which went to the making of *Macbeth* has left no traces in *The Tempest*. The play is singularly free from perishable learning. Even Prospero's farewell speech to the elves and fairies, which Shakespeare drew from one of his favourite books, Golding's translation of the *Metamorphoses* of Ovid (1565–7),[1] has none of the marks of time upon it, and is as much at home in Prospero's mouth as it was in Medea's.

To analyse such a play, as we have done, is to risk misunderstanding. 'Shakespeare,' says Morgann, 'differs essentially from all other writers: Him we may profess rather to feel than to understand; and it is safer to say, on many occasions, that we are possessed by him, than that we possess him. . . . He scatters the seeds of things, the principles of character and action, with so cunning a hand, yet with so careless an air. . . . All the incidents, all the parts, look like chance, whilst we feel and are sensible that the whole is design.' These are truths which no one who has read the fine passage in which they are stated is likely to forget. Some analysis, indeed, there must be, if we are to use our understanding at all. To analyse the working of a plot is always

[1] *Met.* vii, 197 f. (Medea's speech). Shakespeare followed the translation, which is by no means literal. It begins as follows:

> 'Ye ayres and windes, ye elves of hills, of brookes, of woodes alone,
> Of standing lakes, and of the night, approche ye everych one.'

permissible; and, anyhow, we do it. To go further, as we have done, and enumerate the deliberate contrivances by which the feelings of an audience are moved, is a more dangerous adventure, but one not to be declined. The disaster comes when these analyses are substituted for the total impression of the play, which is the chief thing of all, and the last test of the author's art. It is possible to imagine an analysis of *The Tempest* which should resolve it as follows: a wreck upon an island; a high-born magician and his love-sick daughter; an aerial spirit and some dancing nymphs; a monster; some music and songs; several comical misadventures; and three or four spectacles, including a hunt with dogs. But by this method of inventory all that is left to the world of Helen's beauty is, *item* one nose, *item* two lips, *item* two eyes with lids to them, and so forth. These, we see, are not the facts. In such matters it is absolute that 'the Impression is the Fact'.

The critics who found fault with Ariel's songs because they 'contained nothing above mortal discovery', and those others who thought they had discovered Prospero's island in the Mediterranean, though they would have disliked one another heartily, were in the same error. They used their understandings when Shakespeare was addressing himself to their feelings, and thought of details when he was thinking of impressions. This is an error to which editors and all lovers of accuracy in the arts are peculiarly liable; in the close study of detached passages the sense of the whole is lost, and the head goes everywhere before the heart. To imagine, even if it could be shown to be true, that anything is gained to a reader by knowing that Prospero's island was Lampedusa, and lay between Malta and the African coast, or that it was Corcyra, as another critic was equally prepared to prove, is to declare the play, on the whole, a failure. If the island does not convince us that it lies precisely nowhere, the play has missed its purpose, and the total impression which the dramatist was all along striving to produce has not been effected. The island, of course, has neither latitude nor longitude, because Shakespeare gave it none; and this will still be true even if it should one day be discovered, when the lost original comes to light, that the island in this original had a name and a place on the map.

X

OTHELLO, OR THE TRAGEDY OF THE HANDKERCHIEF

To speak for an hour about the tragedy of *any* handkerchief—even when that handkerchief is the charmed and significant lost property of Desdemona—may seem an odd use of one's time. In fact I shall not do so; there are other things which I must talk of first. What I wished to indicate by my title was this: that in my treatment of the play I shall be chiefly interested in the nature of *Domestic* Tragedy, as distinguished from other and more heroic kinds, and in the strange and sinister importance which quite small things—apparent trifles—may assume in Domestic Tragedy: how such things, in the tense and intimate drama of domestic life, may become, symbolically, overwhelming.

I am also profoundly interested in Desdemona's reception of the tragic dilemma in which she was placed. *Should* she—*could* she—have brushed her way through it, with a woman's common sense, and cleared up the childish muddle which in the end destroys her? Or did she show even greater wisdom—a finer perception of what makes life worth living—when she resigned herself, almost without a struggle, to her fate. I am well aware, of course, that I risk here the impertinence of attempting to solve the dramatist's chief problem after he has settled it for himself.

Let me be elementary, and state in the simplest terms the opening situation of *Othello*. The play begins in a street in Venice, late at night. Two men, one a professional soldier, are walking together. The soldier, Iago, is complaining that he has been passed over for promotion, and the staff billet which he thought his due given to a certain Florentine,

Michael Cassio. Their General is Othello, a Moor employed in the Venetian service, and presently they fall to talking of his latest exploit, his elopement, that very night, with the only daughter of a Venetian Senator. Iago grows steadily more bitter and self-revealing, and we begin already to suspect, what is indeed the truth, that, quite apart from his specific grievance against Cassio and Othello, he *hates happiness.* Show him a successful and prosperous man, and his first thought is how delightful it would be to ruin him. Show him two people happy together, and his first idea is how enjoyable it would be to sow suspicion between them, to poison their bliss; and, best fun of all, to do it while passing as their friend.

Suddenly it occurs to him—what an opportunity, that very moment, to give pain all round! Let's have Othello hunted for; let's have him roused; let us

> poison his delight:
> Proclaim him in the streets, incense her kinsmen,
> And, though he in a fertile climate dwell,
> Plague him with flies: though that his joy be joy,
> Yet throw such changes of vexation on't
> As it may lose some colour.

Brabantio, Desdemona's father, is brutally awakened, and with much bustle of servants and torches, sent scouring, half-demented, for his daughter. Enter presently, from another quarter, with attendants, and an answering flare of torches, Othello himself, summoned by the Venetian Senate to a midnight Council of War. Seen on the stage, with the lights moving and weapons flashing, and, in the wavering gleams, the gigantic dusky figure of the Moor, it is a splendid romantic beginning to the play. I need not dwell on the debate that follows. Othello, refusing to wrangle in the street, transfers the issue to the Senate House. There, with an oratory which demands a richer throat than mine, he tells the immortal story of his wooing. Perhaps Brabantio alone is unconvinced. When Desdemona appears, and declares herself his willing wife, the case is closed. Brabantio disowns her; and she prepares to accompany Othello on the campaign against the Turks at Cyprus.

The act ends with a vile analysis by Iago of Desdemona's passion for the Moor. He admits—not here, but later—her virtuous inclinations. But, when all has been conceded, what *is* it, after all, that could conceivably attract a delicately nurtured Venetian girl to this coloured bravo: what but one thing? That she may not herself know this, he is not unwilling to allow, but holds it no sufficient answer. Let her be as well-meaning and as seeming-innocent as you please: she is yet a Decadent, in Nature's hands: Mother Nature!

So ends this rich and astonishingly powerful first act. And now, I should like to comment on it. It will be generally agreed that of all the great tragedies of Shakespeare *Othello* is the most domestic. Seen on the stage, it is, as the plot unfolds itself, liker a tragedy of the modern type than any other that he wrote. And yet, as always in Shakespeare, there are enchantments: intoxications which, even were they within his power, a conscientious modern playwright would probably think irrelevant. Even in this, the most strictly domestic of his professed tragedies, the highest luxuries of Romance are not refused. The first act of the play, which gives the theme, prepares us indeed for the moral deformity of Iago; but it gives also, in designedly overwhelming contrast, the lavish essence of all the romantic stories ever told. Once the hue and cry is started it is a continued tossing pageant of romantic bustle and contention—of gleaming lights and dark masses, of gorgeous vestments and glorious speech. In the principal personages, also, Shakespeare's romantic and aristocratic preferences blaze out. The tragedy may be domestic, but it is no ordinary company, no common family circle that is presented to us. The Moor is a Hero, and the plain citizen's daughter of the old tale has flowered in Shakespeare's hands into the choice and only child of a

Venetian magnifico. Their marriage becomes a question for Senators, an affair of state. There is, lastly, the mysterious and romantic clash of colour: which fascinated Shakespeare, which fascinates all artists: the beautiful Venetian girl thrown up, in lovely and startling whiteness, against the dusky bosom of the Moor.

When we first met Othello he has just been chosen Commander against the Turk, and chosen, not, as Iago would put it, by 'old gradation', by mere seniority, but by general acclaim and the unanimous voice of the Republic. His worst enemy admits that he is a magnificent soldier, the military saviour of the state. Even so, the romantic heart of Shakespeare is not content. The heroism of the Moor must be independent of professional efficiency, and of any rank which governments can bestow. Othello is a Hero in the old, unvarnished, and unashamed romantic sense of one born to do marvels, and fill the world with his name. The accident of love or war may make heroes in the ordinary sense of very ordinary men. But Shakespeare's Othello was never ordinary; he was a predestined Hero in his cradle. He is in the great mould of those barbaric conquerors who swept the East, and threatened Europe with their hordes: a cattle-herd one day, and, by some instinctive and recognizable mastery, a general the next. When he falls at last, by his own hand, a whole world of exploits seems to fall with him.

I think Shakespeare never wrote a finer scene than that of the midnight meeting in the Venetian Senate-house, when Othello answers Brabantio. A born soldier addresses a civilian gathering, and the effect is never in doubt. I am reminded of a well-known conversation in Boswell, which I am perhaps guilty of quoting too often:

We talked of War. *Johnson.* Every man thinks meanly of himself for not having been a soldier, or not having been to sea. *Boswell.* Lord Mansfield does not. *Johnson.* Sir, if Lord Mansfield were in a company of General Officers and Admirals who have been in service, he would shrink; he'd wish to creep under the table. *Boswell.* No; he'd think he could try them all. *Johnson.* . . . No, Sir; were Socrates and Charles the XIIth of Sweden both present in any company, and Socrates to say, 'Follow me, and hear a lecture on philosophy'; and Charles, laying his hand on his sword, 'Follow me, and dethrone the Czar'; a man would be ashamed to follow Socrates. Sir, the impression is universal; yet it is strange.

I will not say that the Venetian Senate wished to creep under the table. But just that impression which Johnson describes seems to have been felt by the Senators when Othello strode forward; and just that impression is felt by us, and, as Shakespeare intended, remains with us. Those opening scenes, after Shakespeare's manner, and indeed the manner of all good playwrights, lightly counterpoise the warring elements of the play. They disclose both beauty and deformity, heroic trust and deadly malice, but still in such proportions as Romance prefers. Evil is as yet but a shadow; the serpent is there, but still outside Paradise. By the close of the first act, Iago notwithstanding, we are raised a long way above the street.

Now this, I wish to remind you, was Shakespeare's purpose. For, observe, that if Othello *was* to be heroic, he had to be heroic in this way, and in the first act. He was there appointed, on a most urgent summons, and with every circumstance of honour, Commander-in-Chief against the Turks, but as Commander-in-Chief he has, as it turns out, nothing to do. The Turkish fleet, we presently learn, has been providentially destroyed in a storm, and when Othello reaches the war area, when he lands in Cyprus, nothing awaits him but to take over the command and resume his interrupted honeymoon. He orders sentries to be mounted; pays a staff visit to the fortifications; and gives a fete to the natives. The rooms of the Castle are thrown open; there are dancing and bonfires; feasting and refreshments are announced from 5 to 11 p.m.

In other hands than Shakespeare's this might well have been an anticlimax. On the contrary, things are just as he wants them. From the beginning of the second act, in strict accordance with this situation, the level of the action is slowly but inevitably lowered from the plane of heroism, on which it began, to the plane of domesticity, on which it is to continue. Not a single adventure is provided except an officers' drunken brawl, nor any soldierly achievement more exciting than the changing of the guard. Everything is favourable to the dramatist's purpose. The whole party goes into barracks, and here also begins the domestic tragedy. Now, as there are no buildings more bleak than barracks, so there is no scandal more bleak than barracks scandal. What, in plain worldly terms, is the position? A disappointed officer spreads the rumour—for that is what Iago now does—that his successful professional rival is in love with the middle-aged General's young wife. A modern playwright, dealing with this theme, would probably accept the bleakness, even welcome it. He would think himself so far successful if he made the play bleak. Shakespeare, rightly or wrongly, like a good Elizabethan, was of another mind, and will nearly always be found, in tragedy, attempting two things at once: to write plays that shall be true to the pains of life, and yet leave us, somewhere, our golden world—plays that, however painful, shall nevertheless be also poetry. This, I repeat, is the strategic value of the first act. No modern dramatist, probably, would ever write such an act. He would not, in fact, begin in Venice at all. He would begin in Cyprus, in the barracks, and we should only hear of Venice.

Shakespeare pays for his first act in some difficulties of time and place which worry nobody except his editors. It was a price he was always prepared to pay. He knew the value of first impressions, even when acquired at the cost of reason. They give to the play, those romantic opening scenes, an initial cast of poetry and of magnificence which even Iago's acid, and the military inaction of the plot, are powerless to destroy. And that, I suggest, is a good reason why *Othello* is one of the greatest domestic tragedies ever written. The freshness that there is in heroism and poetry keeps it sweet.

Iago was no sooner arrived in Cyprus than he got to work. His first object was to bring Cassio into trouble professionally, to shake Othello's confidence in him. His second (and this was luxury) to destroy Othello's married happiness. He succeeds, as we know, in both his objects; and by masterly ingenuity, with diabolical economy, he makes the first intrigue contribute directly to the second. Innocence was never more perfectly trapped.

It has been held by some critics, and uneasily suspected by many more, that, powerful creation as he is, Iago must be judged an unnatural character: *not* because such a person could not possibly exist, but because it is impossible to think of him as at the same time a soldier: all soldiers being notoriously straightforward and simple-minded men. It was an ancient doctrine of the critics, not merely in England but in Europe—you will find it all in Horace—that every category and profession of men has its characteristic form, and that a playwright (for example) commits a serious error if in drawing his characters he strays outside the type. Thus, soldiers should be blunt and hearty men; professors (if so unromantic a character can be endured) should be absent-minded and pedantic; diplomatists should be smooth; and old men should, on the whole, run down the present and praise the past. 'But what is most intolerable', says our sturdy critic Rymer (and he spoke for many), 'is Iago. *He* is no Blackamoor Souldier, so we may be sure he should be like other Souldiers of our acquaintance; yet never in Tragedy, nor in Comedy, nor in Nature, was a Souldier with his Character. Take it in the Author's own words'—and he quotes Emilia's description of the contriver of Desdemona's tragedy—

> some eternal villain,
> Some busy and insinuating rogue,
> Some cogging, cozening slave. . . .

Horace (he goes on) describes a soldier otherwise, as, 'Impiger, iracundus, inexorabilis, acer'. This is certainly a lifelike description of colonels we have known.

Shakespeare, says our critic, *knew* that his character of Iago was inconsistent, but to entertain the audience with something new and surprising, against common sense and Nature, he would pass upon us a close, dissembling, false, insinuating rascal instead of an openhearted, frank, plain-dealing soldier, a character constantly worn by them for some thousands of years in the world. I am bound to say that I find Iago much more of a soldier than his military rival —that 'smock-faced Lieutenant', as Rymer calls him—Michael Cassio. What, to begin with, could be more professional than Iago's grudge against Cassio: a mere staff-officer, promoted over his head—'a great arithmetician'—one who could move troops on paper, by the book, but yet one

> That never set a squadron in the field,
> Nor the division of a battle knows
> More than a spinster.

Have we not all heard this? And he goes on,

> Why, there's no remedy. 'Tis the curse of service,
> Preferment goes by letter and affection,
> Not by the old gradation, where each second
> Stood heir to the first.

Have we not heard this also? Do not just such murmurings go up daily behind the tall windows in Pall Mall? Promotion by influence—by favouritism—and seniority passed over.

And that 'honesty' of Iago, which acquires, as the play goes on, so grim and ironical a value? Did any man ever work harder than Iago to *conform* at least to the outward and orthodox character of the plain blunt soldier—with his constant catchword 'as honest as I am', and his oaths 'by the faith of man'? He even airs the professional soldier's involuntary disdain of the civilian: the Venetians, when we first meet him, are those 'snorting citizens'. And with what ease—how like an old military hand—he arranges that tragic mess-night in the Castle, when Cassio is rooked and ruined!

There is very little comedy in this play. Twice a mild clown shuffles in—finds the atmosphere not favourable—and shuffles out. Only Cassio, in the drinking scene, is allowed for a moment to make us laugh.

Cassio. Well, God's above all; and there be souls must be saved, and there be souls must not be saved.
Iago. It's true, good lieutenant.
Cassio. For mine own part—no offence to the general, nor any man of quality—I hope to be saved.
Iago. And so do I too, lieutenant.
Cassio. Ay, but, by your leave, not before me; the lieutenant is to be saved before the ancient. Let's have no more of this; let's to our affairs.—God forgive us our sins!—Gentlemen, let's look to our business. Do not think, gentlemen, I am drunk. This is my ancient; this is my right hand, and this is my left hand. I am not drunk now; I can stand well enough, and I speak well enough.
All. Excellent well.
Cassio. Why, very well then; you must not think then that I am drunk.

It is impossible *not* to laugh; and we were meant to laugh. But our eyes, in this scene, are on *Iago*, not on Cassio; and which of these two, do you think, is the old soldier? It all works out as Iago had planned. Cassio is provoked into fighting: there is a brawl: the warning bell is rung: the garrison turns out, and Othello with it, and Cassio is reprimanded and dismissed.

Tragedies of domestic life differ from Heroic Tragedy in this: that they are concerned, not with moving ends and moving actions, but, for the most part, with ways and means. That is, no doubt, why they are so terrible to watch: why Othello, for example, is so much more harrowing—it is, at least, to me—than any other of Shakespeare's tragedies. The ends in such tragedies are simple and elemental, like domesticity itself. The horror is in the intricacy of the contrivance—the devilish use which is made of actions and objects protected, one would suppose, from such criminal perversion by their mere simplicity and familiarity. The lost Handkerchief in *Othello*, of which so much is made, is Iago's finishing stroke; and becomes, as the play goes on, a kind of refrain. It has been thought, indeed, by some critics, too trifling for this role of tragedy. It is, on the contrary—and just *because* it seems so trifling—the very *type* of tragic object in the domestic play. Coleridge has a remark on the subject.

Schiller has the material sublime; to produce an effect, he sets you a whole town on fire, and throws infants with their mothers into the flames, or locks up a father in an old tower. But Shakespeare drops a handkerchief, and the same or greater effects follow.

Thomas Rymer was of another mind, and can see nothing in this handkerchief except a warning to 'all good Wives' to 'look well to their Linen'. I quote Rymer, because, writing in the seventeenth century, he preceded the age of Shakespeare idolatry; because he was an honest if wrong-headed man; and because honest abuse of Shakespeare is so rare. On this matter of what he calls the 'Linen' he can scarcely contain himself.

So much ado, so much stress, so much passion and repetition about an Handkerchief! Why was not this call'd the *Tragedy of the Handkerchief*? . . . Had it been Desdemona's garter the sagacious Moor might have smelt a Rat; but the Handkerchief is so remote a trifle, no Booby on this side Mauretania cou'd make any consequence from it.

I am afraid our old critic was blind—as well as a little vulgar. The truth is that in such a play as *Othello* nothing is silly; nothing is too slight or too trifling to become a weapon of devilry. It is this, no doubt, that makes Domestic Tragedy so sinister. The scene is small. The instruments are of necessity so fatally tiny, so deceptively innocent—tittle-tattle, a nod, a whisper, a glove, a handkerchief. On a great scene, among great movements, we are not surprised to find Tragedy, and, when it comes, the exhilaration of great action carries us through. In purely Domestic Tragedy it is difficult to feel this. We are compelled to an almost intolerable concentration.

It was, I suppose, from some sense of these things that men first said: 'Let Tragedy concern itself with the great, let the Tragic Man and Woman be great and noble. As for people like ourselves, and the ordinary men and women we know—let Comedy, merciful Comedy, deal with them.' This, in its largest interpretation, is the natural desire of man to make Death and the Passions romantic, and ordinary life amusing. It does not *refuse* Domestic Tragedy: far from it. But it *does* demand (or rather, I should say, it *used* to demand) that the four walls should not be ordinary walls; or the persons, at any rate, not ordinary persons. Somehow or other, the blood must be raised. This was the tradition in which Shakespeare wrote; and, though now outmoded, it was a great tradition. Modern playwrights, as we know, proceed differently. They write Tragedies preferably about ordinary men and women, and Comedies, with gusto, about the great. The Smiths and Browns make tragedy in a week-end cottage, while Caesar and Cleopatra make comedy among the Pyramids. It is a reversal of tradition, and now a reversal of some standing: and I am not complaining. There are many ways of getting at the truth, and this, no doubt, is one among them. But I miss the Poetry.

It is, or was, a practice, not openly avowed, among professional lecturers on English literature, when they tired of routine, and wished to ease their minds, to announce a course of lectures on Shakespeare. Nothing looks better on a notice-board, and under cover of this title one might speak about almost anything. We talked about Life, and we called it Shakespeare.

In some such a way, I suppose, we have all, at some time, been guilty of the error of taking Desdemona out of her maker's frame, and thinking of her as a dimensional human being, who might have done otherwise than she did. Of course she couldn't. But it is natural enough that we should have these thoughts; that we should sometimes wish, in our more realistic moods, that she could have *seen* a little more of what was happening; have timed her conversations better; have been, as we say, more practical. When we have thought of it again—the dramatic fallacy apart—I hope we have repented. For what was she to do? More and more that sinister Handkerchief is threatening her. She cannot understand Othello's intensity about it—those rolling eyes. Even if it *were* lost! It was to grow and grow, this subtle piece of linen—Chaucer's Venus, you remember, wore a 'subtle kerchief of Valence'—it was to grow and grow until it mingled with her marriage sheets and smothered her.

What should she have done?—if I may pursue that undramatic and merely human curiosity? Here, I have heard it said, was a purely practical difficulty, something that any housewife could meet.

So far as I can see there were only three ways of dealing with Othello's questions about the missing handkerchief—for I dismiss the suggestion once made to me that she might have advertised her loss on the barracks notice board.

(1) *She could tell a lie* (one of those medicinal, those white lies, which ethical casuistry has long permitted, when the lie will do the questioner more good than harm).

She came near to doing this at first: 'Not lost'=*can't* be lost.

Or, (2) *She could have tried to explain:* that, no doubt, was another way.

Or, (3) *She could give it up:* which is, in fact, what Desdemona did: what Cordelia also did, you remember, in no less puzzling circumstances.

Which are we to say was the best?

Before we decide, let me give you, as my conclusion, an example of each of the two methods which she did *not* adopt: let me show them at work. In each case the troublesome object is something in itself quite unimportant. To the tragic handkerchief in *Othello* I will append, for your consideration, two companion trifles: each the occasion or symbol of tragedy.

The first is an *Apple*. The second is a *Bit of String*.

(1) There is a play of Massinger's called *The Emperor of the East*, which has a scene closely modelled on this Handkerchief scene in *Othello*. I will run through it, and leave you to compare. The three principal persons involved are the Emperor Theodosius of Constantinople, the Empress Eudocia, and a grandee called Paulinus—a kinsman to the Emperor and a warm friend of the Empress before her promotion to that rank: indeed her godfather. Paulinus is deadly ill of the gout. The token, which as I say, is an Apple, appears to be historical.

A countryman enters with the apple. After some banter with the courtiers, talking in rude Somerset, he is allowed into the presence, and offers the apple to the Emperor Theodosius. 'Zee here a dainty apple.' The Emperor is amused and delighted: 'It is the fairest fruit I ever saw.' He will send it to the Empress. Here are three scenes, which follow.

Act IV, *Scene* III.—A ROOM IN THE PALACE.

Enter Philanax *with the apple:* (*to Eudocia and maids*)

Phil. From the emperor,
This rare fruit to the rarest.
Eud. How, my lord!

Phil. I use his language, madam; and that trust,
Which he imposed on me, discharged, his pleasure
Commands my present service.

[*Exit* Philanax.

Eud. Have you seen
So fair an apple?
Flaccilla. Never . . .

Enter a Servant.

Eud. You come from
Paulinus; how is't with that truly noble
And honest lord, my witness at the fount,
In a word, the man to whose bless'd charity
I owe my greatness? How is't with him?
Serv. Sprightly
In his mind; but, by the raging of his gout,
In his body much distemper'd; that you pleased
To inquire his health, took off much from his pain,
His glad looks did confirm it . . .

Eud. To him again,
And tell him, that I heartily wish it lay
In me to ease him; and from me deliver
This choice fruit to him; you may say to that,
I hope it will prove physical . . .

Scene IV. A ROOM IN PAULINUS'S HOUSE. Paulinus *discovered in a chair, attended by a surgeon. Enter* Servant *with the apple.*

Serv. My good lord.
Paul. So soon return'd!
Serv. And with this present from
Your great and gracious mistress, with her wishes
It may prove physical to you.
Paul. In my heart
I kneel, and thank her bounty. . . .
Most glorious fruit! but made
More precious by her grace and love that sent it:

To touch it only, coming from her hand,
Makes me forget all pain . . . The emperor only
Is worthy to enjoy it . . .

Re-enter Cleon.

And—cease this admiration at this object—
From me present this to my royal master,
I know it will amaze him . . .

Scene V. A ROOM IN THE PALACE.

Enter Theodosius, Chrysapius, Timantus, and Gratianus, *and later* Pulcheria and Cleon, *with the apple.*

Cleon. Your humblest servant,
The lord Paulinus, as a witness of
His zeal and duty to your majesty,
Presents you with this jewel.
Theo. Ha! . . .

Theo. Further off,
You've told your tale. Stay you for a reward?
Take that. [*Strikes him.*
Pul. How's this?
Chry. I never saw him moved thus.
Theo. We must not part so, sir;—a guard upon him.

Enter Guard.

May I not vent my sorrows in the air,
Without discovery? Forbear the room!

[*Exeunt all but* Theodosius.

Yet be within call.—What an earthquake I feel in me!
And on the sudden my whole fabric totters.
My blood within me turns, and through my veins
Parting with natural redness, I discern it
Changed to a fatal yellow. What an army
Of hellish furies, in the horrid shapes
Of doubts and fears, charge on me! rise to my rescue,
Thou stout maintainer of a chaste wife's honour,

The confidence of her virtues; be not shaken
With the wind of vain surmises, much less suffer
The devil jealousy to whisper to me
My curious observation of that
I must no more remember . . .

Re-enter Timantus.

Theo. Sirrah, upon your life,
Without a word concerning this, command
Eudocia to come to me. [*Exit* Tim.] Would I had
Ne'er known her by that name, my mother's name . . .

Re-enter Timantus *with* Eudocia, Flaccilla, *and* Arcadia.

Can she be guilty?
Eud. You seem troubled, sir;
My innocence makes me bold to ask the cause,
That I may ease you of it. No salute,
After four long hours' absence!
Theo. Prithee, forgive me. [*Kisses her.*
Methinks I find Paulinus on her lips,
And the fresh nectar that I drew from thence
Is on the sudden pall'd. How have you spent
Your hours since I last saw you?
Eud. In the converse
Of your sweet sisters.
Theo. Did not Philanax
From me deliver you an apple?
Eud. Yes, sir;
Heaven, how you frown! Pray you, talk of something else,
Think not of such a trifle.
Theo. How?—a trifle!
Does any toy from me presented to you,
Deserve to be so slighted? do you value
What's sent and not the sender? from a peasant
It had deserved your thanks.
Eud. And meets from you, sir,
All possible respect.
Theo. I prized it, lady,
At a higher rate than you believe; and would not

Have parted with it, but to one I did
Prefer before myself.

Eud. It was, indeed,
The fairest that I ever saw.

Theo. It was;
And it had virtues in it, my Eudocia,
Not visible to the eye.

Eud. It may be so, sir.

Theo. What did you with it?—tell me punctually;
I look for a strict accompt.

Eud. What shall I answer?

Theo. Do you stagger? Ha!

Eud. No, sir; I have eaten it.
It had the pleasant'st taste!—I wonder that
You found it not in my breath.

Theo. I'faith, I did not,
And it was wonderous strange.

Eud. Pray you, try again.

Theo. I find no scent of't here: you play with me;
You have it still?

Eud. By your sacred life and fortune,
An oath I dare not break, I have eaten it.

Theo. Do you know how this oath binds?

Eud. Too well to break it.

Theo. That ever man, to please his brutish sense,
Should slave his understanding to his passions,
And, taken with soon-fading white and red,
Deliver up his credulous ears to hear
The magic of a syren; and from these
Believe there ever was, is, or can be
More than a seeming honesty in bad woman!

Eud. This is strange language, sir.

Theo. Who waits? Come all.

Re-enter Pulcheria.

Nay, sister, not so near, being of the sex,
I fear you are infected too.

Pul. What mean you?

Theo. To show you a miracle, a prodigy

Which Afric never equall'd:—Can you think
This masterpiece of heaven, this precious vellum,
Of such a purity and virgin whiteness,
Could be design'd to have perjury and whoredom,
In capital letters, writ upon't . . .

Eud. Would long since
The Gorgon of your rage had turn'd me marble!
Or, if I have offended—

Theo. If!—Good angels!
But I am tame; look on this dumb accuser. [*showing the apple*

Eud. Oh, I am lost!

Theo. Do you murmur?
What could'st thou say, if that my license should
Give liberty to thy tongue? thou would'st die?
[Eudocia *kneeling points to* Theodosius's *sword.*
I am not
So to be reconciled. See me no more:
The sting of conscience ever gnawing on thee,
A long life be thy punishment! [*Exit.*

Flac. O sweet lady
How I could weep for her!

Arcad. Speak, dear madam, speak,
Your tongue, as you are a woman, while you live
Should be ever moving, at the least, the last part
That stirs about you . . .

Flac. All this pother for an apple!

Well? What about the White Lie? Only a moderate success? We will try the second way then: and see how the method of explanation serves, when some trifle has made a net about the innocent. It is that of Guy de Maupassant's story *La Ficelle.*

It was market day at Goderville . . . Maître Hauchecorne had just arrived at Goderville and was making his way to the market-place, when he noticed on the ground a scrap of string. Maître Hauchecorne, being a thrifty Norman, thought that anything that might be useful was worth picking up: he bent down stiffly, for he was rheumatic, seized the bit of thin cord, and was about to roll it up carefully when he noticed Maître Maladain, the harness-maker, watching him. Maître Hauchecorne, ashamed to be seen by an enemy fumbling in the mud for a bit of string, quickly hid his find under his smock, then in the pocket of his trousers, and pretended to be still seeking on the ground something that he could not find: then he went on his way to market.

Later in the day, when all the peasants were at table in the inn, the beating of a drum was suddenly heard in the courtyard outside, and the town crier proclaimed: 'It is made known to the inhabitants of Goderville and the general public that there was lost this morning between 9 and 10, on the road to Beuzeville, a black leather pocket-book, containing 500 francs. Anyone finding it is asked to bring it to the town-hall at once. A reward is offered. . . .'

They were finishing coffee when a police-officer appeared—'Is Maître Hauchecorne here?'

'Here I am!'

'Maître Hauchecorne, will you be good enough to accompany me to the town-hall? The maire wants to speak to you.'

The mayor, the local notary, a pompous fellow, was awaiting him.

'Maître Hauchecorne, you were seen this morning, on the road to Beuzeville, picking up the lost pocket-book.'

The peasant, dumbfounded, gazed at the mayor, already scared by this suspicion which hung over him.

'*I* picked up this pocket-book?'

'Yes, you.'

'On my word of honour, I have no knowledge of it.'

'You were seen.'

'I was seen. Who saw me?'

'Maître Maladain, the harness-maker.'

Then the old fellow remembered, understood, and grew crimson with rage.

'Ah, he saw me, the villain! He saw me pick up this string, look here, monsieur le maire.' And feeling in his pocket, he pulled out the bit of string.

But the mayor, incredulous, shook his head.

'You cannot make me believe that Maître Maladain, a man whose word is to be trusted, mistook this string for a pocket-book' . . . The mayor resumed: 'After picking up the object, you even went on searching in the mud for some time to see if a coin had fallen out.'

The good man was choking with indignation and fear.

'What a thing to say!'

His protests were vain; he was not believed.

He was confronted with Maître Maladain: he was searched at his own request: they found nothing.

The news spread. As he left the town hall he was surrounded, questioned. And he began to tell the story of the string. He was not believed: they laughed at him. He went about, endlessly telling his story, turning out his pockets to show that he had nothing.

They said: 'Go along with you, you old rascal.'

And he got angry, exasperated, feverish, heart-broken at being disbelieved, not knowing what to do, telling and re-telling his story.

In the evening he went round his village to tell it again to everyone: he met incredulity everywhere. It made him ill all through the night.

Next afternoon, a farm-servant took back the pocket-book and contents to its owner: he had found it on the road, but being unable to read, had taken it home with him to his master.

Maître Hauchecorne heard the news. He set out, and began to relate his story, adding the *dénouement*. He was triumphant.

All day long, he told his tale. He stopped strangers to tell them of it. His mind was now calm, and yet something indefinable troubled him. Everyone seemed amused and unconvinced. . . .

At last he understood. They thought that he had got an accomplice to take back the pocket-book. He was cut to the quick by the injustice of the suspicion.

Once more he began to relate his adventure, lengthening his story, adding new reasons, more emphatic protestations, more solemn oaths. He was believed less and less as his defence grew more complex and his arguments more subtle. He felt it, and lost flesh visibly.

Jokers would now make him tell his story of 'the string' for fun, as one makes an old campaigner tell the story of his battle.

Towards the end of December he took to his bed. He died early in January, protesting his innocence in his death-throes, saying again and again:

'A little string . . . a little string. . . . Look, monsieur le maire, there it is.'

Perhaps, after all, Desdemona was right, and the third method, which she adopted, was the best. When we cease to be believed by those we love best, why go on?

XI

A NOTE ON THE WORLD OF *KING LEAR*

I WAS once asked, and by an undergraduate of this University, how one should *approach* the tragedy of *King Lear*, and I was at a loss for an answer. What should I have said? How does one approach a convulsion of Nature? From what angle? With what stratagems? Under what safeguards? I did suggest, I remember, recovering myself, that this concern about the manner of approach was not, on the whole, the frame of mind in which masterpieces, and, above all, such rending masterpieces as this, are best encountered; that it does not much matter *how* one approaches a great natural upheaval like the tragedy of Lear, but preferably not with one's school prizes under one's arm. My answer, as you may suppose, gave little satisfaction, and yet it was not wholly amiss—being, indeed, only a trifling paraphrase of Lear himself, as he strips to the storm: 'Off, Off, you lendings!' It is the cry of all great tragedy, but nowhere in the literature of the world is the cry so piercing, so practical and imperative as in the drama of Lear.

The command is not easily obeyed, and no reader or spectator is often equal to it. Here's more than three on's are sophisticated! The little arts of life, so painfully evolved, which make us tolerable to one another and even to ourselves, are in a league to resist such tragic denudation: this call of the old king to strip and face the hurricane—to measure oneself with the outcasts under the roof of heaven—to look upon 'the thing itself', that 'poor, bare, forked animal, unaccommodated man'. We are all apt to behave like those sinister callers at Gloucester's castle in the play, as darkness fell, and the bleak winds began their howling:

> Shut up your doors, my lord; 'tis a wild night:
> My Regan counsels well; come out o' the storm.

This civilized timidity, this instinctive repugnance to the primitive scene, the moral and physical humiliations, and the desperate challenge of such a play as *King Lear*, is stronger, no doubt, in some races than in others. In this island Nature still holds her own, though in a losing battle; we have not yet parted company with the unaccommodated life, with the simplicities of the wide places and the windy heaths, where man looks small. The French find it harder. Excellent as they are at the social anatomy of man, and little, in that mood, as they leave him to be proud of, they cling more than we do to their acquirements, and are noticeably more reluctant to take the freedom of the elements. No Frenchman could have written *King Lear*; and of those few who know it, still fewer can endure it. Twenty-two years ago the *Tragedy of King Lear* was performed at Paris at the Théâtre Antoine (it can seldom have been performed since), and when I say that it had not a good press I use the language of diplomacy. 'The most second-rate maker of melodramas', said Maeterlinck (a devout admirer of the play), 'the least ambitious writer of Vaudevilles', would have been disheartened at the reception given by the most eminent French critics of the day to the greatest of English tragedies. One or two writers stood out against the general vituperation, and reminded their readers that, whatever might be thought of *King Lear*, the author of *Hamlet* and *Othello* was at least entitled to respect. But they were alone in their forbearance. M. Émile Faguet declared in the *Débats* that, unlike the majority of Shakespeare's tragedies, in which coarse and hideous melodrama *is* mixed with artistry, *King Lear* is little more than coarse and hideous melodrama with the art left out. 'Save for a few beauties of lyrical eloquence in the famous tenth scene, and some fairly profound philosophical reflections (if we take the trouble to fathom them) in the mad scene proper—all of which is quickly told—with these exceptions', wrote M. Faguet, 'all the rest is no more than a heap of stupid crimes, foolish horrors, and idiotic vices. It is what I call (he goes on), using a perhaps unjust and undoubtedly hybrid term, *bruto-tragedy* or *bruto-drama*. . . . With the exception of the short portions which I have reserved nothing is easier to put together. There is not a man in Europe at the present time (and I would even include the last 100 years) who would be capable of writing *Hamlet*, or *Othello*, or even *The Tempest*. But almost anybody, no matter who, could write *King Lear*, with the exception of a few passages, which, all taken together, would barely fill a page. The characters, with their summary and almost childish psychology, all of a piece in their ignominious brutality, do not even arouse our curiosity.'

This is startling. But Paris was on the critic's side, and could the circumstances be repeated, Paris and every normal Frenchman would be with him still. We can see, of course, what Faguet meant. The play is primitive from its first origins. It is founded on an incident as childish as you will, a nursery story of early man. The oldest boy will give away his things: and who loves him most? Who is most friends with him? The shy little girl comes off badly. Frenchmen have been by no means alone in complaining of this. William Cory, a good Englishman, found Lear 'such a fool in the beginning' that he 'couldn't take any interest in him'. He should have gone further, and should have remembered also how many of the older tragedies of the world, because Tragedy by its nature deals with unreason, distortion, and excess, are founded on stories and episodes no less childish and perverse.

This primitive groundwork is matched, in Shakespeare's play—and, among all the versions of the story, in Shakespeare's play alone—by the primitiveness of its people and of the world in which they live. This is the principal charge in Faguet's indictment. Shakespeare, he supposed, would have civilized his matter—his persons and his scene—if he could. He did not know that what Shakespeare, in fact, set out to do was just the contrary. Shakespeare designed to make the simple story credible: to frame for these self-willed children of nature, for their primitive passions and brutalities, a world in which they should seem not too palpably unreal. On this design he has expended all the resources of his mind and art, and with a success so overwhelming that, simply as a feat of dramatic anthropology, this picture of a remote and pagan Britain surpasses all other reconstructions. The theatre is unchristened Nature, and on this vast and designedly vague terrestrial platform, roofed by a malignant sky, a royal household—with that freedom to be publicly and brutally selfish which primitive royalty confers—works out the strategical manœuvre of its appetites.

The historical scene is that mythical and Trojan Britain, fabled centuries before Christ and while Rome still had kings: there is a European background of kingdoms and courts, of wars and confederacies. It is a world, however, as Shakespeare represents it—as, with unusual care, he laboured to represent it—ruled directly by the elements and the heavenly bodies, and more remotely by deities not even as yet discriminated. The theology of Lear is thrown at us, after Shakespeare's manner, in the first scene. He turns from Cordelia, and appeals, as he always does when humanity fails him, to the Powers above. What are they? He takes his oath

> by the sacred radiance of the sun,
> The mysteries of Hecate, and the night,
> By all the operations of the orbs
> From whom we do exist and cease to be.

These are the highest powers he knows.

Next comes in Gloucester, and we are in a world of eclipses, star-blasting, and planet-striking. Shakespeare, like his audience—like any audience—loved omens, and when he has tragic business, habitually prepares us in this way. But in *King Lear* we are never out of them, or of the fear of them: it is a world made of omens: living by them as, we are told, all primitive communities do. Some instructed persons there were who pretended to explain these prodigies by natural causes. But Gloucester, plain man, is not convinced.

Though the wisdom of nature can reason it thus and thus, yet nature finds itself scourged by the sequent effects.

Gloucester it is true, was old-fashioned in these matters, and was laughed at for it by the livelier of his sons. Much has been made of young Edmund and his disillusion. He is the New Age, agnostic, and rails in good style at 'the excellent foppery of the world, that, when we are sick in fortune . . . we make guilty of our disasters the sun, the moon, and the stars; as if we were villains by necessity, fools by heavenly compulsion, knaves, thieves, and treachers by spherical predominance, drunkards, liars, and adulterers by an enforced obedience of planetary influence; and all that we are evil in, by a divine thrusting on.' He is the only person in the play who flouts the primitive faith (though some, like Goneril, ignore it), and it is the first count in Edgar's accusation of him: 'False to thy gods, thy brother and thy father.'

That faith is Fatalist, and without the only comfort that Fatalism can bring. They are Fatalists without repose. We meet them, it is true, at a time of crisis; but with no other time are we concerned. These Pagans walk in fear. Demons lie in wait for them; plagues in the sky hang 'fated o'er men's faults'; good and evil contend in still unresolved celestial battles; chaos is for ever but just averted. There is a divine and feared caprice. Gloucester, when he appeals to Heaven, coaxes and wheedles his divinities. Only Lear stands up and thunders at them; and *his* voice is more commonly directed, not to any Pantheon, but to the Elements and to Nature herself—this Nature, so despotically powerful, so sudden and cruel.

You may remind me that Lear swears by Gods, and by the

Gods of Greece and Rome. I reply that he swears, on such occasions, by too many Gods. Johnson observed this. In the first scene he swears in turn by Hecate, Apollo, and Jupiter: on which last oath Johnson protests: 'Shakespeare makes his Lear too much a mythologist: he had Hecate and Apollo before.' They may be regarded, these invocations, as either an Elizabethan negligence or a natural relic of his Trojan origins. In any case this God or that, mere departmental deities, could never have contented Lear. Towering in his passions, as lunacy dilates him, he addresses by preference the Universal Goddess: 'Hear, Nature! hear, dear Goddess, hear!'

The superiority and majesty of Nature is figured in the Heavens, and when Lear addresses them he speaks not on his knees, but erect, as a subject member of their confederacy, and even—and in a most famous and pathetic passage—as their *contemporary*.

> If you do love old men, if your sweet sway
> Allow obedience, if yourselves are old,
> Make it your cause; send down, and take my part!

Young ingratitude is triumphing: will the ancient Heavens take sides?

This theme, of the heartlessness of youth to age, dominates the play. It is more than the ingratitude of children—'discarded fathers' and 'pelican daughters'. Shakespeare, with a true instinct, and with consummate art, extends it, as the play goes on, to Youth and Age in general, and makes it the most bitter and fatal quality of the primitive world which he depicts. 'In Lear', says Coleridge, 'old age is itself a character.' It is here, above all, that the sometimes uncomfortable parallelism of the double plot—the story of Gloucester and his inhuman son—does best service. Lear's case is not, then, isolated, but takes the intended status of a possibly universal cruelty, of a law of nature. The play is riddled with the contempt of

Youth for Age: 'idle old man'; 'old fools are babes again'; 'bind fast his corky arms'. The observant Edmund noted this feature of his world and hoped to rise by it: 'The younger rises when the old doth fall.'

Here, as it seems to me, is intended to be the only credible explanation of Goneril and Regan, if monsters are to be explained. The source and spring of his daughter's conduct to Lear is not so much the ingratitude of children to a father as a barbarous and primitive inability to look on Age without contempt. Lear, as I understand him, sees this, though not always.

> Ask her forgiveness?
> Do you but mark how this becomes the house:
> 'Dear daughter, I confess that I am old;
> Age is unnecessary; on my knees I beg
> That you'll vouchsafe me raiment, bed, and food'.

'*Age is unnecessary.*' There you have it: the law of the primitive community: of the Jungle: of the Pack. Even Cordelia, if I may dare to say it, sinned a little from youth—simply from not properly understanding the feelings—or, if you like, the weakness—of Age. This is a version of that unfeelingness of youth which Gray the poet once noted, and noted without blame:

> I am very sure, I have seen the best-tempered, generous, tender young creatures in the world, that would have been very glad to be sorry for people they liked, when in any trouble or pain, and could not, merely for want of knowing rightly what it was themselves.

Something of this may be found in Cordelia, before her marriage. She has 'l'esprit géometrique', and will not play the old man's game. 'So young, my Lord, and true', needs some interpreting. True she was, but—oh!—so young!

It is not to be wondered that in such a play the public has always cherished Cordelia, who is, in fact, and was, I believe, to the dramatist, no more than a piece of daughterly mechanism in the first act, and a gleam of daughterly sunshine in the last. It is tempting to make too much of Cordelia in a play which contains only three women, and two of them fiends. We do not wholly despair of a world which contains her. She was kind, and honest, and affectionate, and *ordinary* (a great point, that); beautiful, too; and all the poor people in the play had lost their hearts to her. It is tempting to be sentimental about her and give to a play which deals in so much wilder and sterner emotions this softer, less British, and more English cast. It is tempting, but it will not do. When Lear comes in with Cordelia in his arms, the play is still—as it always has been—with Lear. The great heart of the people is motherly: it is always whispering 'poor things'. But neither the tragedy of Lear, nor of Hamlet, nor of Othello, nor of Macbeth, is to be understood by that part of an audience which can only dab its eyes: which would make all tragedies tragedies of the Handkerchief.

This is the play, says Hazlitt, truly, 'in which Shakespeare was most in earnest'. We see it not only when his powers were most wanted and most spent—in Lear's great agony and illumination—but in the unusual care with which he makes his setting. By this I do not mean that he avoids, or attempts to avoid, what is called anachronism. Oswald is an Elizabethan portrait: Kent is put in the stocks: there is the usual easy and unembarrassed jumble of ancient and contemporary things. But as it has been said, 'not all the Elizabethanism in the world can temper this play's ancient savagery with a contemporary civility'. How cunningly, it has been noted, Shakespeare has handled the weapon of vagueness. Nothing, as Bradley says, seems to be anywhere, and this gives also the feeling of vastness, 'the feeling not of a scene or particular place, but of a world'. 'This world is dim to us, partly from its immensity, and partly because it is filled with gloom. It is called, we are told, *Britain*; but we should no more look for it in an atlas than for the place called Caucasus, where Prometheus was chained.'

Gloucester cites 'the wisdom of Nature'. By this he means that natural philosophy of his time, that concern about the '*causes* of things', which so permeates this play that few scenes of any length will be found in which this consuming interest is not represented, from the passionate probings of Lear into the hidden virtues of things, and the mysteries and maleficences of being and generation, to the insistent play by the Fool with the popular curiosities of the same great theme. Shakespeare in these matters goes always to work the same way; and if an effect of art or atmosphere is to be made all his agents must contribute at their appropriate level. When the Fool jests about the oyster and his shell, and asks why the snail has a shell for his house, and the nose is in the middle of the face, he is still trafficking in the popular margins of that same 'wisdom' which draws from Lear some of his most exalted utterances.

The system of 'Nature' which is found in this play, its natural philosophy, was not hard for Shakespeare to come by. It had descended with singularly little change through the medieval encyclopaedists to his own time, and was substantially the natural philosophy of his age. One manual in particular we may suppose him to have known. Certainly whoever opens Batman's *Bartholome* finds himself almost startlingly immersed in the prose background of the physical world of *King Lear*, from the highest reaches even to the oyster and its shell. The domination of Nature in *King Lear*, and the helplessness of humanity which accompanies it, is linked in Shakespeare's handling with a pervading interest, sometimes idly and sometimes seriously expressed, in the *secrets* of nature, and the search for hidden causes.

All blessed secrets
All you unpublish'd virtues of the earth,
Spring with my tears! be aidant and remediate.

So Cordelia cries by the bedside of Lear. But this quest is always appearing, and is evidently suggested by Shakespeare as having a fascination proportionate to the ignorance of the time. There is a passage in Act III, sc. 4, which bears on this, and has never been explained. It is one of the Storm scenes, before the hovel on the Heath, and Gloucester comes searching with a torch, to offer food and shelter. Lear will not be parted from poor Tom; he has questions to ask him.

Gloucester. Our flesh and blood, my lord, is grown so vile,
  That it doth hate what gets it.
Edgar. Poor Tom's a-cold.
Gloucester. Go in with me. My duty cannot suffer
  To obey in all your daughters' hard commands:
  Though their injunction be to bar my doors
  And let this tyrannous night take hold upon you,
  Yet have I ventur'd to come seek you out
  And bring you where both fire and food is ready.
Lear. First let me talk with this philosopher.
  What is the cause of thunder?
Kent. Good my lord, take his offer; go into the house.
Lear. I'll talk a word with this same learned Theban.
  What is your study?
Edgar. How to prevent the fiend, and to kill vermin.
Lear. Let me ask you one word in private.
Kent. Importune him once more to go, my lord;
  His wits begin to unsettle.
Gloucester. Canst thou blame him? [*Storm still.*
  His daughters seek his death. Ah! that good Kent;
  He said it would be thus, poor banish'd man!
  Thou sayst the king grows mad; I'll tell thee, friend,
  I am almost mad myself. I had a son,
  Now outlaw'd from my blood; he sought my life,
  But lately, very late; I lov'd him, friend,
  No father his son dearer; true to tell thee, [*Storm continues.*
  The grief hath craz'd my wits. What a night's this!
  I do beseech your Grace,—

Lear. O! cry you mercy, sir.
Noble philosopher, your company.

What does all this mean? Why 'philosopher'? and why these questions? I will tell you, for the commentators have never really explained it. We are here in that 'wisdom of nature' of which Gloucester spoke, or as the manuals called it 'la sapience de la nature'. Shakespeare had been looking into it: reading up some anthropology—in order to see what the old world of *Nature* was. Lear mistakes the Bedlam for a professional wise man, acquainted with the secrets of Nature and the reasons of things. Now all kings formerly kept such a philosopher, who was technically so called, just as they kept a Fool and other court officers. Lear, we are to suppose, had a philosopher when he was king, and is now adding him to his mock court. The practice goes back to remote antiquity. Alexander and Aristotle; the fabled King Boctris and his philosopher Sidrach; Virgil, turned necromancer, and the young Prince Marcellus; Daniel and the Biblical king; Merlin and Vortigern; Michael Scott and Barbarossa; Dr. Dee and Queen Elizabeth: the conjunctions are endless. Frederic Barbarossa, who did things thoroughly, had a *staff* of 'philosophers'—with that title—whose well-understood function it was to examine and report on the causes of Nature. The more successful added magic, divination, and prophecy to their accomplishments.

In the Middle Ages one of the most popular forms of instructive reading was the dialogue or catechism, in which one of these celebrated philosophers instructed his royal pupil. The pupil asks questions about every sort of thing—including, of course, 'the cause of thunder'—that was a stock question. They were wondering about it in the time of Cambuskan, if Chaucer may be trusted:

> As soore wondren somme on cause of thonder,
> On ebbe, on flood, on gossomer, and on myst,
> And alle thyng, til that the cause is wyst.

The philosopher always answers. Indeed in one of these books a 'philosopher' is *defined* as 'a gentleman who answers the questions put to him'. We begin to understand now what Lear was after, and the cause of his persistence, and we begin to see that Shakespeare had *read* to some effect.

Perhaps the most popular of these dialogues was the so-called *Book of Sidrach*, philosopher to King Boctris of Armenia, or, as it was also entitled, the *Sapience of Nature*, the Wisdom of Nature. It was early translated into English, and four versions of it, one complete, were published in London in the sixteenth century. There is little doubt that Shakespeare had seen one of them. The questions asked cover the range of nature, and the answers are by no means dull. Here are some of them.

The cause of things: Why is it we blow on our hands to warm them, and on our soup to cool it?—the old puzzle of Aesop's fable and La Fontaine's.

Why have clocks in churches? To give the hour of prayer, because God loves regularity.

Can any human being hear the music of the spheres? Only children hear it when they smile in their sleep.

What is the cause of eclipses?—Why do the stars go out?—Why are the planets seven?—Why has the snail a house?

Ought one to beat one's wife? Not if she is a good wife—it will be enough to speak to her: if she is one of the bad ones beating will be useless.

Why did God make the world? To populate the sky, and fill the vacant places of the fallen angels.

Why has God exposed man to so short, so harassed, and so diseased a life? To have done otherwise wouldn't have been fair to the Devil.

What is the proportion of men to birds, beasts, and fishes? For every person there are 100 beasts, without counting vermin, and for every beast 1,000 birds and 10,000 fishes.

Ought one to be always adoring God? No! one must work for one's living.

Love at first sight? It is a mistake to fall in love. When you see a beautiful woman you should say with compunction 'Blessed be God who made so fair a creature'.

What is the cause of gaiety and high spirits? The kind of food you eat has a great deal to do with it.

The spirit of the age—can we overcome it? Yes: by thinking of something else.

Ought one to drink wine or water? Wine is a precious and worthy thing.

Shall the elect in Heaven remember the ills of their lengthy life? Yes, do the Knights not tell over to their friends the story of their campaigns?

Two of the questions in this selection, you will note, recur in the scene of *King Lear*, where the Fool, reversing things, puts the 'reasons of nature' to his master:

> Why does one's nose stand i' the middle on's face?
> How does an oyster make his shell?
> Why has a snail a house?
> Why are the seven stars no moe than seven?

Shakespeare, it will be seen, with an eye to the primitive colouring of his play, has chosen to give the lighter side of his researches to the Fool. Some of the ancient questions were still going on in the seventeenth century, with answers not unlike what I have just been reading. One question Lear asked just after he had done with his philosopher, while his mind still ran on causes: 'Is there any cause in Nature that *makes* these *hard* hearts?' The Books of Wisdom, I am afraid, have no good answer to this question. The only answer is the Tragedy itself, on which I have detained you so long.

XII

SHAKESPEARE'S ENGLISH[1]

IF you had asked an English writer of the sixteenth century what his difficulties were, and in particular why England had been so slow to produce masterpieces since Chaucer, after the usual authors' talk about the scarcity of patrons and the neglect of merit—having eased his mind on this eternal topic—he would almost certainly have named, as the chief obstacle to literature, the embarrassing state of the English language. There was no fixed standard, he would have complained; no accepted grammar, or spelling, or pronunciation, or accent; and, to add to these native troubles, there was an intolerable influxion of new words. That schooling of language which goes on in the places where youth is taught—which tames language but at the same time makes it manageable—all the strength of that discipline was expended on Latin, which was still the language of Europe and the verbal medium of the professions. Latin had its well-tried grammars, its dictionaries, its long-thought-out rules of diction and composition; it had models for everything, and was thoroughly well taught. The modern vernaculars, with the single exception of Italian, were unripe for this status. They could point to few received models, and were growing so fast that neither dictionary nor grammar could keep pace with them. What English a man had depended much more than now on his surroundings and his mother wit, and the schoolmaster was only casually concerned. A boy, of course, might be lucky. It made some difference, I fancy, to young Spenser's English studies to have sat under Richard Mulcaster of the Merchant Taylors'

[1] Society for Pure English Tract XXIX, based on a Lecture delivered at the Royal Institution on 5 February 1926.

School, and Shakespeare, in his turn, may have been favoured. But Holofernes raises doubts. That Shakespeare was taught grammar, even English grammar of a kind, is plain, and that he took a young man's revenge for it. Holofernes actually thinks in grammar: as a lady approaches, 'a soul feminine saluteth us', he says. He even gets his terms of abuse from it, which seems a stretching of function: 'thou consonant!', he cries, as Moth enrages him. Shakespeare was to do what he liked with English grammar, and drew beauty and power from its imperfections. In the rankness and wildness of the language he found his opportunity, and exploited it royally, sometimes tyrannically. But the complaints which have come down to us from the critics and linguistic reformers of the century are not to be dismissed. Whatever genius might do with it the language needed policing. It was from no eccentricity that Ben Jonson in his old age—*elementarius senex*, as he ruefully remarks, a greybeard among the school-books—laboriously compiled, in the generation after Shakespeare's death, an English grammar. Among his cures for the distempers of his countrymen this ranks as one.

In England, of course, things are never as bad as they seem. Our practice is always so much better than our theory. But the trouble persisted, and was felt, long after the Elizabethan effervescence, not only by grammarians but in the highest walks of literature. So fine an executant as Dryden, in the last years of his life, announced it as a national scandal that we had yet no English prosody, nor 'so much as a tolerable dictionary, or a grammar; so that our language is in a manner barbarous'.[1] Nothing but a government subsidy, he thought, could put the matter through, and what English government would subsidize a committee of writers and grammarians? Addison, Swift, Pope, and their friends were still discussing, in the next century, the Standard English Dictionary of the future, and Addison at one time had even thoughts of supply-

[1] *Discourse Concerning Satire*: *Essays*, ed. Ker, ii. 110.

ing it, marking passages in Tillotson for the purpose. But the work was too hard for that group. Thirty years later—fifty years after Dryden's protest—the same complaint can still be heard: our language is without test or standard, said Warburton in 1747, 'for we have neither GRAMMAR nor DICTIONARY, neither Chart nor Compass, to guide us through this wide sea of Words'.[1] Yet the language of that time seems settled enough. It is an odd story, and helps to explain what used to puzzle me, and may, I suppose, have puzzled others, why Samuel Johnson, when he produced his English Dictionary and Grammar in 1755, became a great man at once. Merit alone will not explain it; there is a history behind that acclamation. He had made, without help either from government or from committees, the book that England had been waiting for and intermittently demanding since the sixteenth century. The long chase, it seemed, was over. Our rebel language was caught up at last. Leviathan was hooked.

The linguistic disorder of the sixteenth century was variously felt. It was felt less in prose, the plainer sorts of prose especially, which were protected, as always, by the common sense of daily use. Our historians of literature, in their devotion to a great 'Period', are inclined to suggest that there was both a poetical and a prose revolution in the latter years of Elizabeth. A poetical revolution there certainly was, of a swiftness when it came (though it had been painfully prepared) only twice to be matched in our literature; but in prose, as I read it, nothing nearly so drastic. The improvement, much crossed by individualism and eccentricity, was almost normal. It was poetry, as we should expect, that had suffered most from the want of standards. For though poetry can get along without much grammar or schooling, accent, at least, is fundamental to it. There must be some agreed

[1] *Preface* to his *Shakespeare*, p. xxv.

expectancy of the ear. Now that is precisely what was wanting, and, except in popular song, had been wanting in England for nearly two centuries. The language had moved away from the old poetical forms and phrases. Pronunciation and accent were at open civil war, and the main business of Tudor poetry was to reconcile them. It took two generations to compose that difference, and a third—which was partly Spenser's and partly Shakespeare's generation—to ratify the peace and finger out the new concord. Rhythm conquered its material, and the ear and the tongue re-established correspondence. Yet the victory was not complete, and we are often reminded, as we read the great Elizabethan poets, that the new paradise of sound had been won from chaos.

Another and a more attractive chaos engages our attention: the Elizabethan language and its world of words. I hesitate in these days to praise anarchy in any form, but in the kingdom of language, and even of literature itself, there are worse things. One exhilarating result of the linguistic licence of the century was, in its latter years at any rate, a period of almost complete linguistic freedom. What had at first been an embarrassment became, as wits grew nimbler, the sport of sports. For one long generation the language rioted in the use of all its limbs, and of every prehensile toe and finger. There had never been such a time for the bold employers of words, and there never will be again. Of course there were usages, and some usages were thought better than others; but they were most of them uncertain, and they were not easily enforced. The good poet, says Richard Puttenham in 1589, will not follow any English that may chance to be in use. He will follow the language which is spoken in the king's court, or in the good towns and cities within the land, rather than the English of the marches and frontiers, or of port towns, or yet of universities, or of the rustic uplandish people, or of mere craftsmen. And this English, moreover, shall be Southern English. Our poet will not take the terms of

Northern men, such as they use in talk, 'whether they be noble men, or gentlemen or of their best clarkes, all is a matter': nor in fact any speech used beyond the river of Trent, nor yet 'the far Western man's speech'. But he will take 'the usual speech of the court, and that of London and the shires lying about London, within sixty miles and not much above'.[1]

This, in fact, is roughly what was done, and by dramatic poets like Shakespeare, who wrote for London, must have been done inevitably. But the latitude allowed was still royal. Court English itself was far from uniform. The noblemen and gentlemen of whom Puttenham speaks carried their county about with them on their tongues. Sir Walter Ralegh, the pink of elegance, spoke Devon all his life, as Shakespeare, no doubt, spoke Warwickshire. It was even a matter of pride among some of our patriots that this should be so. 'The copiousness of our language,' says one of them, 'appeareth in the diversity of our dialects; for we have court, and we have country English, we have Northern and Southern, gross and ordinary, which differ each from other, not only in the terminations, but also in many words, terms, and phrases, and express the same things in divers sorts, yet all right English alike.'[2] This hearty gospel is as far as possible from the old mistaken theory, which modern philology has destroyed, the theory that a language can and should be fixed; that the first duty of a language is to have a polite usage, and that everything else should be for ever impolite; that a civilized language should be commended, like a fashionable club, rather for its power to exclude new-comers than for its willingness to inspect and admit them. The Elizabethans lived before the vogue of this academic theory of language

[1] *The Arte of English Poesie*, bk. III, ch. iv: *Eliz. Crit. Essays*, ed. Gregory Smith, ii, 150. The book is anonymous, and the ascription of it to this or another Puttenham is disputed.

[2] Richard Carew, *The Excellency of the English Tongue* (*c.* 1595): *Eliz. Crit. Essays*, ii. 291–2.

(though one can see it coming), and we, by a similar good fortune, live after its decline. It is a point of community between the Elizabethans and ourselves of which I think we are conscious, and nowhere more warmly than over the language of Shakespeare.

For the first quality of Elizabethan, and therefore of Shakespearian English, is its power of hospitality, its passion for free experiment, its willingness to use every form of verbal wealth, to try anything. They delighted in novelties, and so exultingly that prudent word-fearing men became alarmed. The amusing thing is that even the alarmists are unable to deny themselves the very contraband they denounce; in this matter of language they were all smugglers. Thanks to this generous and unlicensed traffic we discover a quite astonishing number of words, introduced, apparently, by the Elizabethans, which to-day we could not do without. We observe also—what is not without some practical interest for us—the impossibility of predicting, of any new words at any given moment, which of them were going to last.

There are three interesting lists, apologetic or contemptuous, of sixteenth-century innovations to which I should like to refer, more especially as two of them seem partly to have escaped the notice of the *Oxford Dictionary*. Those two we owe to what literary history has never any difficulty in supplying, I mean the quarrels of authors. There is (1) Richard Puttenham's list of words of which he had himself been guilty; (2) Thomas Nash's list culled with loving care from the pages of his antagonist, Gabriel Harvey; (3) Ben Jonson's anthology of the Bad Poet's language in *The Poetaster*.

Puttenham apologizes, in the year 1589, for such liberties as these: *scientific*, *idiom*, *method* and *methodical*, *function*, *refine*, *compendious*, *prolix*, *figurative*, *impression*, *numerous* and *numerosity*, *harmonical* and *harmonically*, *penetrate* and *penetrable*, *savage*, *obscure*, *declination*, *delineation*, and *dimension*. He apologizes, and yet makes bold to think that 'strange and unaccustomed' as some of these words may be, they have their uses in the language. Of certain other and more questionable innovations—*audacious* (for 'bold'), *facundity* (for 'eloquence'), *egregious* (for 'great' or 'notable'), *implete* (for 'replenished'), *compatible* (for 'agreeable in nature')—his defence, he acknowledges, must be less hearty.[1] The author of *The Arte of English Poesie* is a figure of some importance in Elizabethan literature. He had thought about things, and his book was timely and influential. It was read by Shakespeare when it came out, and has been classed, on the evidence of language, among his early favourites or books of reference by that excellent scholar the late Mr. H. C. Hart. A number of the words which Puttenham cites are pre-Elizabethan; it is interesting to find them still open to challenge. But *scientific* and *idiom* are new, like his modern use of *method* and his application of *savage* to human beings. He extended the meaning, also, of *figurative*, *penetrate*, and *penetrable*, and was the first, so far as we know, to use *numerous* and *harmonical* of verse.[2] The vocabulary of Shakespeare shows some coincidence with Puttenham's list. *Function*, *method*, *penetrate*, *penetrable*, *dimension*, and *obscure*, as well as *audacious* and *egregious* (in its better sense), are all employed by Shakespeare, and some of them he treats with marked favour. It is even possible that he took over from Puttenham the new word *ode*.

I turn to Thomas Nash, who, in the year 1592, cannot moderate his contempt for such upstarts and abnormalities as these: *conscious* ('conscious mind'), *egregious* (in the laudable sense), *jovial*, *energetical*, *rascality*, *materiality*, *artificiality*, *fantasticality*, *addicted to theory*, *perfunctory discourses*, *amicable terms*, *effectuate*, *novellets*, *notoriety*, *negotiation*, *mechan-*

[1] *The Arte of English Poesie*, bk. III, ch. iv: *Eliz. Crit. Essays*, ed. Gregory Smith, ii. 151–3.

[2] One of Puttenham's unsuccessful probationers, the word *Politien*, meaning a statesman or public minister, he describes as 'at this day usual in the Court and with all good Secretaries' (*ibid.*, bk. III, ch. iv).

ician.[1] It is a striking list, from which I conclude that as a lexical prophet Nash was farther from infallibility than Puttenham. Harvey, no doubt, was something of a magpie in his passion for verbal odds and ends; there are other phrases in the list (not quoted here) which deserved their pelting. But he had runs of luck. Of the words cited nearly half seem to have been used by Harvey for the first time. *Artificiality* (by the *Oxford Dictionary* first recorded in Shenstone, 1763); *conscious* (first noted by the same authority in *The Poetaster*, 1601); *energetical* (in the *Oxford Dictionary* post-dated 1603); *extensively* (not noted in the *Dictionary* before 1645, or in Harvey's sense before 1730); *fantasticality* (Nash himself, as Harvey points out, has 'finicality'); these, with *novellets* and *notoriety*, are all, it would appear, Gabriel Harvey's own bantlings.[2] They have lasted a great deal better than Nash foresaw.

Nash and Harvey are vivacious duellists. But the struggles of the new diction are even more vividly displayed in the last scene of Jonson's *Poetaster* (1601), a scene partly founded on the *Lexiphanes* of Lucian. Crispinus, the Bad Poet, who is in fact Marston, is obliged, like Lucian's wordmonger, by the rough process of an emetic, to part with the more outrageous portions of his vocabulary. The monstrosities thus disgorged seem many of them now surprisingly innocent: *retrograde*, *reciprocal*, *defunct*, *spurious*, *damp*, *clumsy*, *chilblained*, *clutched*, *strenuous*, *puffy*, *conscious*.[3] (This last, it will be remembered,

[1] Nash, *Strange Newes* (1592): *Eliz. Crit. Essays*, ii, 241–2. The expressions are cited from Harvey's *Foure Letters* (1592). Of *egregious* Nash asserts that it is 'never used in English but in the extreame ill part'. Yet Marlowe and Shakespeare both use it on occasion like Puttenham and Harvey. Nash's own *carminist* and *carminical*, which Harvey retorts against him, have missed recording in the *Oxford Dictionary*. A *carminist* is a poet, and poetry is the *carminical art*. See *Eliz. Crit. Essays*, ii. 275.

[2] *Negotiation* is earlier; it is first recorded in the *Oxford Dictionary* under 1579. But Harvey was using it by 1580 (*Letter-Book*, 142). Of *jovial* in its modern sense (to be found in Shakespeare's *Macbeth*) Harvey furnishes an earlier example than the Drayton passage (1596) in the *Dictionary*.

[3] *Reciprocal* was a comparatively new word; it is used by Shakespeare in *King Lear*. *Defunct*, also, was favoured by Shakespeare; he has it as a noun

Nash had already excommunicated.) There were other words, of course, more deserving of ridicule.

> *Horace*. How now, Crispinus?
> *Crisp*. O.—*obstupefact*.

This monster is one of them, and with *ventositous*, *oblatrant*, *fatuate*, *turgidous*, and *prorump*, may be thought to have fully justified Crispinus's martyrdom.[1] But all alike are rejected, from *retrograde*, the first word, to *obstupefact*, the last. In this particular kind of insight, as a broker in verbal 'expectations' or the futures of words, Ben Jonson, it would appear, was no more gifted than Nash. Yet he had given his mind to these things. One of his last public jokes, it may be recalled, turned on a verbal habit of his old enemy Inigo Jones. Jones had two pet words; *conduce* was one, and *feasible* was the other. From this alone it may be seen that Jones was of the class from which we instinctively make chairmen; which angered Ben. In his *Tale of a Tub* (V. ii) the great architect, disguised as Vitruvius the Cooper, uses both the words twice in thirteen lines.

'It would form an interesting essay', says Coleridge, speaking of the *Poetaster* passage, 'or rather series of essays, in a periodical work, were all the attempts to ridicule new phrases brought together, the proportion observed of words ridiculed which have been adopted, and are now common, such as *strenuous*, *conscious*, &c., and a trial made how far any grounds can be detected, so that one might determine beforehand

---

and as an adjective, and coined *defunction* and *defunctive* from it. In the *Oxford Dictionary* he is credited with the first use of it as an adjective, but the usage is pre-Shakespearian. *Spurious* was a new-comer, some two or three years old in 1601, as were *strenuous*, *chilblained*, and *puffy*, all fathered by Marston. *Clumsy* has an odd history. It begins to appear, says the *Oxford Dictionary*, about 1600, but is found in none of the dictionaries or word-books before the eighteenth century. Marston introduced it, and was rewarded as we have seen. It is not in Shakespeare.

[1] None of these words survived.

whether a word was invented under the conditions of assimilability to our language or not. This much is certain, that the ridiculers were as often wrong as right; and Shakespeare himself could not prevent the naturalization of *accommodation*, *remuneration*, &c.; or Swift the gross abuse even of the word *idea*.'[1] It is the moral which I have been trying to enforce. I have been collecting for some years the material for such an inquiry, and some of the essays which Coleridge asked for are even drafted. But the grounds of success and failure in the verbal world are hard to find, and, though prolonged comparison does something to disinter them, the quest is still elusive. The Elizabethans made the usual mistakes about innovations, but they might, on the other hand, have made a great many more. They were saved by their executive freedom, their experimental gusto, and their genuine and widespread feeling for word-creation. The good writer in those days, and especially the good poet, had to be something of an etymologist and more than usually a phonetician, and there is evidence that the best of them took this trouble. The sensitiveness of Shakespeare to the quality, the habits, and the history of the words he plays with is a trained gift.

The new words from the Latin which overflowed into English in the sixteenth century, and more particularly at this time, underwent, of course, some change in the process, but as a rule the least possible. The verbs were simply dealt with, and by a method peculiar to English among the modern languages of Europe. They were commonly formed, not, as in French, from the present stem, but from the passive participle. The expression, 'a church *dedicate* to God', which would now be conscious archaism, seemed normal in the sixteenth century, and implied, to an English ear, a verb 'to dedicate'. On this easy model most of the new verbs were made. The nouns, the Graeco-Roman especially, took longer

[1] *Lit. Remains*, ii. 273.

to acclimatize. We can see them coming in, at first as conscious foreigners, *criticus*, *poema*, *epitheton*, *theoria*, Ascham's *idioma*, Sidney's *energia*, Shakespeare's *statua*, *effigies*, and *pyramis*. *Theoria* quickly becomes 'theory', and *poema* becomes 'poem', taking the place, for this purpose, of the older 'poesy'. The *criticus* of the doctors passes into *critic* in Shakespeare's *Love's Labour's Lost*, that playground of the new language, and to show what he is about he gives it twice. In the same piece the solemn *epitheton* of Foxe and Holinshed appears as a Don Armado pomposity, having already begun its progress, through *epithete* and *epithite*, to the modern form. *Idiom*, *energy*, *statue*, *pyramid* all emerge, and the usual stir begins; the more lively of the new-comers collect a family. *Critic* gives birth to *critical* (another of Shakespeare's passing gifts, this time in *A Midsummer-Night's Dream*), and *energy* starts off with *energical* and *energetical*, which by the middle of the next century have lightened themselves and become *energic* and *energetic*. Words are in this respect like persons. The more of a household they can assemble, and the more alliances they can make in the country or language of their adoption, the less danger they run of dying out. They make a little clan which holds together. Many single and lonely new-comers perished and left no mark, or lingered obscurely until later revivalism found them out. I think—at random—of Shakespeare's *militarist*, not recorded again before 1860; of *devastate* and *devastation*, never really accepted until the nineteenth century; of *insane* and *insanity*, Elizabethan formations which did not escape Shakespeare, but lay almost idle in the dictionaries for nearly two hundred years.[1]

There was much waste, of course, in this word-ferment of

[1] *Effigy* cannot fairly be included among these neglected words, though its freedom came late. Its ancestor *effigies* is first recorded in Shakespeare, and he used it only once. Its fate was peculiar. It came to be used almost exclusively in the plural, or in the phrase *in effigie*, forms doubtfully suspended between English and Latin. Its long quarantine ran out in the Age of Anne; the first example of plain *effigy* which the *Oxford Dictionary* records is in a paper by Steele (1713).

the age. There always is when one experiments, and the Elizabethans were experimenters born. The learned Englishmen of the Renaissance, Sir Thomas More and his contemporaries, had deliberately enriched our language from Latin sources, and from that example, in part, the later fecundity derives. But the situation had changed. Luxury had followed want, and the last race of the Elizabethans, secure from verbal poverty, turned self-indulgent. What had once been a necessity had by Shakespeare's time become a game. You tried a thing to see what happened. The process might be fortunate, or it might not. It produced *turgidous*; but it also produced, and by exactly similar means, both *strenuous* and *conscious*. It supplied, from 'domus', as a new word for mansion, the unnecessary *dome*; but this misfortune is amply compensated by such admirable discoveries as *orb* and *event*. It was responsible for *obstupefact*, but by precisely the same method achieved *degenerate* and *defunct*. Even the failures played their part, as in genuine experiment they so often do. The first attempt to secure a new word is always more likely to be a failure than a success, but it holds the ground for the moment and gives a chance of doing better. The important thing, as it seemed to most Elizabethan writers, was to secure the word in *some* form. *Turgidous*, it appears, won't do. Very well. Yet, but for *turgidous*, we might never have had *turgid*, and the language of criticism would have been so much the poorer.

I have always, myself, had a feeling for *prorump*, one of Jonson's rejects. It covers so admirably the whole area of aggressive and precipitate action. 'The meeting prorumped': how much bolder and vivider than 'the meeting broke up' or 'dispersed in disorder'! I could even face the possibility of a substantive *prorumption*; if its form is irregular so is the action which it denotes. 'You have been guilty, sir, of a grave prorumption of duty.' In the Services, I believe, the word would go far. The intrusive -m gives force and body to it, like the 'suetty' b in Lamb's spelling of plum(b)-pudding.

It is in the plays of Shakespeare that the general movement may best be studied. He was, by every sign—indeed the evidence is overwhelming—in the first rank of the advance, and of all its members the most exuberant; an experimenter always, though in the diction of his time; making his language as he went along. Only the Americans to-day profess to do this. I am concerned for the moment with the simplest part of the business, with vocabulary, and am well aware how much richer and more intricate a subject is his creative handling of phrase and idiom. But we must walk before we run, and though I shall not wholly ignore it, that larger theme must be for other discourses. A book on Shakespeare's language, considered in its whole extent, is badly wanted. I have waited for so long for some one else to write it that I have decided to wait no longer, and, incited by Mr. Onions, am now writing it myself. But I must not confound this lecture with the book.

We speak freely of the verbal inventions of Shakespeare, and have excellent reason for doing so. With the *Oxford Dictionary* to guide us, and Mr. Onions's *Glossary*, we even make lists of his inventions. It is an attractive, but, at the best, a conjectural exercise, for colloquial evidence has disappeared, and even the *Oxford Dictionary* is founded on selective reading. To say definitely that Shakespeare or any other author invented a word or a phrase is to say, very often, what we cannot know. We are better equipped, it is true, for such inquiries than we have ever been, or than any other nation at the present day; where our ancestors only guessed (where a Frenchman still guesses) we can sometimes risk assertion. But Dr. Johnson's warning holds. 'Authors,' he says, 'are often praised for improvement, or blamed for innovation, with very little justice, by those who read few other books of the same age. Addison himself has been so unsuccessful in enumerating the words with which Milton has enriched our language, as perhaps not to have named one of which Milton was the author.' The language of Shakespeare has been more thoroughly registered and more curiously scrutinized than that of any other English writer, and his less considerable predecessors are still imperfectly known. There must be many words and idioms first recorded from his writings which he was not in fact the first to use, however his sanction may have recommended them. Yet when all admissions are made the record for one man is still enormous. Among the expressions first known to us from Shakespeare, because he either coined or introduced them, I note these: *aerial*, *auspicious*, *assassination*, *bare-faced*, *bump*, *castigate*, *clangor*, *compact* (sb.), *compunctious*, *conflux*, *control* (sb.), *countless*, *critic* and *critical*, *crop-ear*, *denote*, *disgraceful*, *distrustful*, *dog-weary*, *what the dickens*, *dwindle*, *dress* (sb.), *ensconce*, *eventful*,[1] *exposure*, *fair play*, *fancy-free*, *fitful*, *foppish*, *foregone conclusion*, *fretful*, *gibber*,[2] *gloomy*, *gnarl* and *gnarled*,[3] *heartsore* and *heartwhole*, *herblet*, *hurry*, *home-keeping*,[4] *hunch-backed*, *ill-got* and *ill-starred*, *illume* and *relume*, *immediacy*, *impartial*, *lack-lustre* (Shakespeare was the first to make free use of this prefix), *lapse* (vb.), *laughable*, *leap-frog*, *leer* ('the leer of invitation'), *lonely*,[5] *lower* (vb.), *misplaced*, *monumental*, *outfrown* (with many other *outs*, *out-Herod Herod* among them: this vivid cast of phrase is first illustrated in his works), *pedant* and

[1] A Shakespearian coinage, used once, in *As You Like It*, and not heard of again until Johnson included it in his *Dictionary*, citing only this passage. It came into use in the last quarter of the eighteenth century.

[2] The *Oxford Dictionary* has no rceord of the word between *Hamlet* and Cowper's *Odyssey* (1791).

[3] First found in *Measure for Measure* ('gnarled oak'), and not again until the nineteenth century.

[4] The word is in *The Two Gentlemen of Verona*. No one else seems to have used it until Miss Mitford very appropriately revived it in 1826.

[5] In *Coriolanus*; but Sidney has *loneliness* much earlier. It was taken up by Milton.

pedantical,[1] *perusal*, *predecease*, *on purpose*, *repair* (sb.), *reword*, *road* in our sense and *roadway*, *savagery*, *seamy* (the 'seamy side'), *skimble-skamble*, *superflux*, *sprightful*, and *sportive*. Omitted from this list are a great number of words less serviceable to the general language, though with glorious impromptus and choice compounds among them, many of them formations occurring only once, and never meant for circulation. They served, which was all he asked, for their immediate purpose of expression.

Much more has been written about the verbal audacity and word-creativeness of Shakespeare than about another power of his, more remarkable even than his gift of formal invention—I mean his genius in the manipulation and development of meaning. It is exercised with habitual felicity on the commonest expressions in the language, and is an abstract of that shaping power exerted daily and almost unconsciously by every nation of speakers. The miracle is to see so communal an engine in private hands. Shakespeare possessed this power in a degree never approached before or since by any Englishman, or perhaps by any individual mind; he seems, as he employs it, to be doing the work of a whole people.

Let us accept, for the moment, the provisional *data* of the *Oxford Dictionary*, and turn over the results. So far as history can yet tell us, he was the first of our writers to speak of 'cudgelling one's brain', 'falling to blows', 'breathing' a word, and 'breathing' one's last. It is in Shakespeare, on this same testimony, that firearms and debts were possibly first 'discharged', persons 'humoured', letters 'directed', and unkindness 'buried'; there also for the first time men 'bury' their faces in their cloaks. The stirring people of his plays 'drink healths' and 'pledges', say 'done!' to a bargain, 'lay odds' and play 'the ten', 'grovel' or 'hedge', are 'spiritless'

[1] Both words are first found in *Love's Labour's Lost*. A generation later English writers were still using the forms *pedanti* and *pedanty* (Ital. *pedante*). *Pedantry* was arrived at in the eighteenth century through *pedantery*, from Ital. *pedanteria*, which is in Sidney.

and stare on 'vacancy', or 'reel' along the street: all, possibly, for the first time in print. On the same reckoning they were the first public characters to call the world 'dull', to speak of the 'acts' of a play, to find speeches 'flowery' and plain faces 'homely', to be 'fond' of each other, to 'wear their hearts on their sleeves', to have 'balmy slumbers', and lie on the 'lush' grass. No earlier writer is yet known to have spoken of a man's toes 'looking through' his shoes, of the 'makings' of a thing, of an 'abrupt' answer; of 'men of note' and of sending a 'note'; of 'the minute' drawing on; of 'backing' a horse; of things that 'beggared' all description; of 'catching' a person up, or 'catching' a meaning or a cold; of painting from 'the life'; of being 'bright' in the sense of cheerful, or of being 'sick' of a thing; of 'sealing' one's lips; of 'returning' thanks, or a present, or an answer; of 'getting' information, or 'getting' an ailment; of 'getting clear' of debt, or of a ship, or 'getting' aboard, or back, or off, or on ('Get on thy boots'). For the first time, also, we have literary authority to call a vehicle a 'conveyance', a ship's crew a 'company', anything that happens an 'event',[1] and a road a 'road'.[2]

It is an endless and, of course, quite speculative theme on which I have embarked, and it has taken me far from my Latinisms. Much that lexicography would seem to ascribe to Shakespeare in default of other parentage belongs, no doubt, to the colloquial life he knew so well. But he had a genial share in the business, and his contribution is the more impressive because it has merged so easily in the common fund. I should like, if I had time, to show him at work on certain words—such a word as *orb*, which he made his own, and which the poets took over with his enrichments. A simpler example is *accent*. It was a sixteenth-century word, in use in

[1] Whence his coinage *eventful*.

[2] *Road* in this new sense is first found in *1 Henry IV*, and was evidently liked by Shakespeare. Its normal meanings were 'roadstead' and 'inroad'. Cotgrave (1611) defines *voleur* as 'a robber, or highway theefe; and 'an inroder, or a roadmaker'.

didactic and rhetorical connexions. Shakespeare at first employed it in the ordinary way, but soon began to play upon it; when we speak of a Scotch or an American 'accent' we are enjoying a usage which Shakespeare possibly began. He had a favour for the word, and presently, in a great passage, lifted it bodily from the lecture-room and threw it clear. The first stage of the liberation may be seen in *King John*:

> Pardon me,
> That any accent breaking from thy tongue,
> Should scape the true acquaintance of mine ear.

The last is in *Julius Caesar*:

> How many Ages hence
> Shall this our lofty Scene be acted over,
> In States unborn, and Accents yet unknown?

It is an interesting question how far Shakespeare's English was coloured by his native dialect, and betrays, or exploits, the speech of Warwickshire. The possibilities have been stated with characteristic judgement by Henry Bradley,[1] but so as almost to inhibit assertion. A London dramatist would normally avoid provincialism, and advices such as Puttenham's would tell him nothing that he did not know. Yet a considerable free trade between the central and southern dialects is implied in that pronouncement, and an existing liberty among writers (however much he might deplore it) of drawing expressions from provincial sources. Rusticities apart, provincialism was hard to fix between Trent and Thames. Puttenham is urgent for a standard and a geographical limitation because the first was unsettled and the second shadowy. The presumption would seem to be that Shakespeare might use a Warwickshire expression if it suited him.

The evidence for Shakespeare's use of dialect has been last and best collected in Mr. Onions's *Shakespeare Glossary*.

[1] In the last chapter of *Shakespeare's England*.

Some of the evidence is remarkable, as Henry Bradley acknowledged, and parts of it have still to be assimilated by Shakespeare's editors. Mr. Onions has restored or justified more than one rejected reading on the evidence of the midland dialects alone.[1] Shakespeare's interest in dialect is limited. He will parody the speech of a neighbouring nation—Scotch, Welsh, or French—in the common manner of the stage, but he seldom reproduces rustic English. He prefers to suggest, with a colouring word or two perhaps, the country homeliness. He had none of Spenser's interest in dialect, and was apparently unmoved by the current theory of the English Ronsardists, who regarded dialect, in our nineteenth-century manner, as a virgin plot or unsifted treasury of poetic language. His nearest approach to this party is in his flower-names, which he fetches, as a rule, from his own country-side.

But here, as in so much else, he is opportunist. He judges a word by what it can do for him, now; and if he wants it he takes it, wherever it comes from. Most of the words he brings from dialect are rather forcible than pretty, and have more pith and village realism than poetry. I think, to give examples, of *aroint*, *ballow*, *bawd* (a hare), *batlet*, *blout*, *bemoil*, *basimecu*, *dowle*, *geck*, *gallow*, *grow to*, *muss*, *mobled*, *minnick*, *nayword*, *potch*, *pother*, *runnion*, *squinny*, *tarre*. *Dwindle* and *drumble* are comelier recruits, and *dwindle* he may be said to have established in literature. There is a notable triplet in *Macbeth*,

> dwindle, peak and pine,

of which we owe perhaps two-thirds to Shakespeare and the midlands. All three have lived, and *peak* has been *pine*'s partner ever since. He has phrases also, and epithets, with the telling mark of the people on them—*nook-shotten*, *blood-boltered*, *the be-all and the end-all*, *to burn daylight*: all four first found in Shakespeare, and some at any rate of midland origin. But I approach, and perhaps have passed, the allowed

[1] See his Introduction, p. iv.

limits of speculation in a region of inquiry where the syllogism hardly runs.

The fertility and happy-go-luckiness of Elizabethan English, and the linguistic vitality of its greatest master, are apparent in a field of language which is sometimes overlooked: I mean, in the making of words by derivation. Alongside the importation of new expressions, and the occasional culling of the dialects, there was in progress, like some exuberant and native principle of health, another movement: a revival of derivative word-making, and, as a part of the process, a deliberate resuscitation of some of the oldest creative practices of the language. We have been trained by a line of schoolmasters to handle those significant atoms, the prefix and the suffix, with a certain conservatism and etymological respect. By Shakespeare and his contemporaries, on the other hand, they appear to have been regarded rather as so much loose material, capable of almost infinite combination with the bodies of words.[1] First, the foreigners were set free. The etymological tradition which had confined certain prefixes to words of French or Latin origin was swept aside, and *dis-* and *re-*, for example, with their vast potentialities, were released for general service, and licensed to make native connexions at their employers' will. It became possible not only to *disable*, to *dismiss*, or *disapprove*, but to *distrust*,[2] to *dislike*, or to *dishearten*, and to *rebuild* now seemed as regular as to *re-edify*.[3] A large number of new words were formed in this

[1] Certain inhibitions, however, remained. The Elizabethans, for example, felt as we do about the suffixes *-ation* and *-ative*, that their place is with verbs of French or Latin origin. The only exception in *-ative*, as the *Oxford Dictionary* reveals, is the word *talkative*, which somehow stumbled into the language in the fifteenth century. The check on *-ation* was defied in the eighteenth century, when first *flirtation* (1718) and then *starvation* (1778) broke the rule. But they have had few followers, at any rate on this side of the Atlantic.

[2] The *Oxford Dictionary* cites Lydgate, *c.* 1430, for *distrust*, but seems to regard it as an accident. It is certainly an odd formation at that date.

[3] *Renew* (after L. *renovare*), which occurs in Wyclif, Trevisa, and others, is regarded by the *Oxford Dictionary* as a chance anticipation of later practice Before the end of the sixteenth century such combinations are rare.

way; of the numerous words in *dis-* which appear in our dictionaries the majority were made in Shakespeare's lifetime.[1] The French prefix *en-* shared the general liberation, and was freely attached to English forms.[2] Sidney's *endear* (which Shakespeare uses), Spenser's *embosom* and *encloud*, Shakespeare's *ensnare*, *ensear*, *enmesh*, *enfreedom*, and *ensky* may be named with *engird*, *embody*, *enkindle*, *enlink*, *enfold*, and *entangle* as typical products of the new licence.

In these, as in most of the novelties and verbal fashions of the time, Shakespeare took his swing. *Dishearten* he may have coined, as he improvised *disbench*, *disedge*, *dispark*, and perhaps *dis-seat*. *Recall* is his, and *respeak* and *reword*; he is soon at home among these simple freedoms.[3] The enfranchised prefix *en-* he is even inclined to overwork, like many a poet since. There is a line in the Folio version of *Othello* (II. i. 70) where the trick goes crazy:

> Traitors ensteeped to enclog the guiltless keel.

Both *ensteeped* and *enclog* are words made for the occasion, and never used again.

I said that in the Elizabethan development of this derivative word-making there was an element of revival, and revival of some of the oldest practices of the language. I had in mind

[1] Obadiah Walker asserts, a generation later, that *un-*, *dis-*, and *re-* 'may be prefixed at pleasure' (*Some Instructions concerning the Art of Oratory*, 1659, p. 31). Yet the new words in *dis-* have not lasted well. Many were nonce-formations which in the brave Elizabethan manner served their maker and died: *disbowel* and *disgarboil*, *discloak* and *dis-spur*, *dismaiden* and *diswench*, *dislove*, *dislive*, *diswit*, *diswont*, *disweapon*, *disbishop*, and *dispriest*. There were also *disfriendship*, *diskindness*, *disholy*, and *disworkmanship*, and, luckier than many, *distaste*. Warner fell in love with the trick, and ventured *diskingdom*, and, less happily, *disyellow*. Sylvester also, as with every meanest aid to word-creation. *Disknown* and *dis-self* came as easy to Sylvester as *rewhelp* and *reyoung*.

[2] This prefix was set free somewhat earlier than the others. It was Skelton, I believe, who first enlarged its range; he made a cult of it. I note, among his performances, *enturf*, *englad*, *ensand*.

[3] Gabriel Harvey, with his usual quickness, is among the word-makers here. *Retell* and *requicken*, both used by Shakespeare, are first recorded in his works.

among other things (for I must limit my examples) some native English suffixes, long potent in word-making, and potent still, but fallen idle for want of enterprise when the Elizabethans took them up.[1] There was a hunger at that time for adjectives, a poetical craving to describe. Every pattern and mould of epithet was dragged out and inspected, and it was found that some of the oldest patterns were among the best. They were therefore revived, and the affection spreading, as such things do, there was tumbled into the language by one poet or another, from Sackville and Golding to Spenser and Shakespeare, a whole race of new adjectives on the old model. *Heedful* and *heedless*,[2] *gleeful* and *luckless*,[3] *direful*[4] and *hapless*, *sapless*[5] and *senseless*, *cloudless* and *hopeless*, *grateful*[6] and *soulless*, *pleasureless*, *fitful*, *distrustful*, and *fretful*,[7] may stand as not unfavourable specimens of the new mintage, with *finny*, *fleecy*, *bosky*, *briny*, *horsy*, *snaky*, *gloomy*, *dusky*, *shiny*, as a small but impressive handful from the mob of new-comers in *-y*.[8] It was a notable addition to expressive power, and a timely draft on native resources.

[1] I am indebted, in this matter of suffixes, to the pioneering labours of H. C. Hart, who did so much for the study of Shakespeare's English. See especially his editions of the Three Parts of *Henry VI* in the Arden Shakespeare. Hart was always breaking new ground, but sometimes, as he confessed, labelled his finds a little hastily. His lists and some of his statements need correction.

[2] *Heedless*, *hapless*, and *pleasureless* are first found in Golding's *Ovid* (1565–7). This antedates slightly the record of *hapless* in the *Oxford Dictionary*, and alters considerably the history of *pleasureless*, first cited there under the year 1814.

[3] First recorded in Sackville's *Induction* (1563).

[4] *Direful* followed hard on *dire*, another Elizabethan word, and had been overworked by the time of Jonson's *Volpone* (1605).

[5] One of Shakespeare's coinages, used twice in *1 Henry VI*, and never again. It was taken up by Peele, who was much given to this kind of adjective; he seems, among other exploits, to have been responsible for *cloudless*.

[6] The word *grateless* deserves recording as a courageous Elizabethan attempt to match the irregularly formed *grateful*. It did not survive the century.

[7] The last three adjectives are all Shakespeare's, and the list might be prolonged (by *changeful*, *spleenful*, *countless*, *dateless*, &c.).

[8] Spenser was the chief executant in this way. He had a liking for these simple adjectives. *Finny*, *briny*, *horsy*, and *shiny* seem all to be his, and he gave his favour to *fleecy*. *Bosky* is first found in Peele, *snaky* in Turbervile, and *gloomy* in Shakespeare.

These adjectives are generally regarded by literary students when they consider them at all, as chance products of a fertile age, and a great many of them, no doubt, were made quite casually. It was easy enough; a man once started could turn them out for ever. Shakespeare made them and forgot them, coining *disgraceful*, for example, at the beginning of his career, and never using it again. But there was more than casual fertility in the matter, and, if I labour this a little, it is because the case is typical. The reason why so many of these adjectives were made was partly, no doubt, because they were needed, but still more because they were fancied: because Golding and Spenser, among others, had deliberately cultivated them, and because Shakespeare and all the other young expression-hunters of the nineties had Golding's *Ovid* and Spenser's poems in their heads.[1] It is amusing to see how smartly they borrow each other's finds; how Golding's *heedless* and *careless*, for example, reappear inevitably in Spenser and Shakespeare, and Sackville's *luckless* in all three; or how Spenser and Marlowe almost dispute by their nimbleness as connoisseurs the Shakespearian paternity of *gloomy*. For they were collectors as well as inventors, and hunted words and verbal patterns as bibliophiles hunt first editions [2] I have been tempted even to think that they researched, and dived for specimens in the past, for the older group, at least, was antiquarian. How otherwise explain the resurrection, shall we say, of *careless* and *shapeless*,[3] which disappear from

[1] It is hardly realized how large a proportion of the adjectives of these three classes, with their contingent nouns and adverbs, was formed in the Elizabethan period. Of the collaterals of *heed*, for example, *heedful*, *heedfully* and *heedfulness*, *heedy*, *heedily*, and *heediness*, *heedless* and *heedlessness* are all, apparently, Elizabethan. Many other words would give similar results.

[2] The virtuoso of the business was Sylvester, and his works its rag-bag. Yet ought one to sneer at a poet whom Milton studied, and who coined, perhaps, such words as *deathless*, *star-spangled*, and *princeling*?

[3] *Careless* is as old as the Cædmonian *Exodus*, but no example is cited by the *Oxford Dictionary* between Layamon's *Brut* (*c.* 1205) and Lyly's *Euphues* (1579). Golding, however, had it some twelve years before. Of *shapeless* the *Oxford Dictionary* has no record between 1300 and 1587, and the revivalist once more is Golding. He had in fact used it twenty years earlier.

written record for three or four centuries, and reappear simultaneously—in Golding? Or the return of *kindless*, untraced between Orm's *Ormulum* and Peele? Or of *deathful*, unrecorded for three centuries before Sidney? Or of *dewy*, which vanishes after Anglo-Saxon times until the sixteenth century, and is relaunched if not restored by Spenser? The explanation, I suppose, is that these words were re-invented; but that they should have been re-invented, and by this particular group of writers, proves all that need be claimed.

It has been observed that these writers tend to group their verbal fancies, and to give them out in clusters, two or more at a time. It is a weakness of poets, and is a sign either of novelty or of affectation, and frequently of both. Shakespeare succumbed less often than most to this temptation. But I quoted a moment ago a line from one of his maturest tragedies in which he makes public love to a prefix; for a similar attention to a suffix I may cite this passage from perhaps his earliest play:

> Weak shoulders, overborne with burthening grief,
> And *pithless* arms, like to a wither'd vine,
> That droops his *sapless* branches to the ground:
> Yet are these feet, whoes *strengthless* stay is numb, . . .
> Swift-winged with desire to get a grave.[1]

Here, in three lines, are three adjectives of the new vogue, and one of them invented for the occasion.[2] But such wantonness is rare, and he very soon outgrew the grosser weaknesses of the current styles. The run of adjectives in *-y* in *A Midsummer-Night's Dream* is iteration of a different sort, and has

[1] *1 Henry VI*, II. v. 10–14.

[2] Cp. *3 Henry VI*, II. vi. 18, 23–25: *luckless—bootless—cureless—merciless*. He had a fancy for *ruthless* at this time; it comes in all the *Henry VI* plays, and five times in the third (*3 Henry VI*, I. iv. 31, 156; II. i. 61; V. iv. 25, 36). Hart asserts that the three adjectives above are new; but *pithless* and *strengthless* are pre-Shakespearian. Shakespeare was well enough satisfied with *sapless* to repeat it in IV. v. 4 of the same play, and he has *strengthless* again in *2 Henry VI*, *Lucrece*, and *Venus and Adonis*: all early works.

a special meaning and appropriateness there. *Rushy*, *unheedy*, *sphery*, *brisky*, *barky*, and, in some twenty-eight lines between Oberon and Puck (III. ii. 356–84), the further complement of *starry*, *testy*, *batty*, *wormy*, are drops in that delicate rain of nicely calculated rusticity with which Shakespeare has sprinkled the language of this play. Four of the nine, *sphery*, *brisky*, *batty*, *barky*, he made for the purpose. There is a simplicity about this suffix which pleased the pastoral Spenser, but, like all simplicities, it was easily overdone. Ben Jonson thought Marston clownish with his *clumsy*, *barmy*, *puffy*, 'outlandish terms'. Shakespeare is more tactful, and his fun is gentler. But *brisky* is a joke; *starry* is mated with the archaic and ludicrous 'welkin'; and even *sphery*, though Milton found it here and placed it in the firmament of *Comus*, can hardly by its maker have been intended seriously. It is Hermia's 'eyne' that are sphery, as it is the 'welkin' that is starry, and the adjectives incur some part of the rusticity of their nouns. So in *Antony and Cleopatra*, when he invented *plumpy* for the triumvirs' drunken song, archaic 'eyne' keeps up the note:

Plumpy Bacchus, with pink eyne (II. vii. 120).

There is a place in *Henry V* where Shakespeare may be seen in the very act of experiment, trying a likely formation on his ear. You will find there, in the space of sixty-seven lines, four words, *vaultage*, *rivage*, *sternage*, *portage*, of which all but the second are inventions, struck out to the chosen pattern as he went along. *Rivage* and *sternage* come within four lines of each other in the stirring Chorus to Act III, where he describes the departure of the fleet for France, and *portage* is in the tenth line of the following scene. It is interesting to note that, though this scene is on land, Shakespeare's mind still lingers with the Chorus and the English shipping in the Channel, and the eyes of the resolute English infantry are conceived as peering from their heads like braces of cannon in a ship's ports. The image and the form together might seem to warrant the suggestion that the forty-five lines from the beginning of Act III were written at a sitting.

This quick and eager play with the bodily elements of words is a characteristic of all his work. In no detail of his language is there fixity; its forms and even its senses are in transition to the end. In his later writing, when his language is outraced by thought, he risks all for meaning, and rather than be stopped or impeded in his course dares everything that the flux of forms made possible. Few of the class of words thus hurled on paper—his *actures*, and *embracures*, and *insistures*, his *sortances* and *sonances*—have lasted well, or, indeed, outside his works, deserved to last. But he would not have minded. He made them for his own use, and they served and (since we study him) still serve his turn. The success of his experiments in language is to be tested artistically, as we criticize the furnishing of a room or the hanging of a picture. The question is not, 'Does this suit universally and for ever?' but 'Does it suit here and now, in the identical situation in which we find it?' The life of Shakespeare's verbal experiments is often limited to their birthplace, but as often, it may be supposed, their creator contemplated no other life for them. This is how we should all like to make our language, quite freshly, just as it is wanted. Shakespeare comes nearer to that ideal than any other writer, perhaps, who ever lived.

I had hoped, in this paper, to say something about the recovered facility in word-compounding which distinguished the writers of the Elizabethan age, which deformed their prose as much as it adorned their poetry, and which led Shakespeare to his 'proud-pied April' and his 'heaven-kissing hill'. But it is a subject too capacious to be dealt with in asides, nor is it now to be handled in a postscript. I preferred, when it came to the point, to discuss the humbler method of derivation, because it is so often ignored. As to the Latinizing with which I began, an opportunity may perhaps be given me, in some future Tract, to pursue the literary and colloquial fortunes of that invasion, as it surged above and below stairs: not only in the upper world of rhetoric and poetry, but in that underworld of the Latinist movement of which Dogberry is at once the saint and martyr.

INDEX

PRINTED IN GREAT BRITAIN
AT THE UNIVERSITY PRESS, OXFORD
BY VIVIAN RIDLER
PRINTER TO THE UNIVERSITY